RELIGION AND THE NORTHERN IRELAND PROBLEM

JOHN HICKEY

RELIGION AND THE NORTHERN IRELAND PROBLEM

GILL AND MACMILLAN

BARNES & NOBLE BOOKS
Totowa, New Jersey

First published 1984 by
Gill and Macmillan Ltd
Goldenbridge
Dublin 8
with associated companies in
Auckland, Dallas, Delhi, Hong Kong,
Johannesburg, Lagos, London, Manzini,
Melbourne, Nairobi, New York, Singapore,
Tokyo, Washington

© John Hickey 1984

First published in the USA 1984 by
Barnes & Noble Books
81 Adams Drive
Totowa, New Jersey, 07512

Library of Congress Cataloging in Publication Data
Hickey, John.
    Religion and the Northern Ireland Problem.
    Bibliography: p. 147.
    1. Christianity — Northern Ireland.
    2. Northern Ireland — History — 1969.
    3. Northern Ireland — Religion.
    I. Title.
BR796.3.H53 1984   303.6'2'09416   83-26612

    0 7171 1115 6 (Gill and Macmillan)
    0-389-20448-X (Barnes & Noble)

Hickey, John.
Religion and the Northern Ireland problem.
1. Christianity and politics.
2. Northern Ireland — Politics and government.
I. Title
941.60824   DA990.U46

Print origination in Ireland by
Galaxy Reproductions Ltd
Printed by
Biddles Limited

For Susan

DONEGAL

BALLYCASTLE
COLERAINE
ANTRIM
DERRY
DERRY
BALLYMENA
LARNE
MAGHERAFELT
STRABANE
CARRICKFERGUS
COOKSTOWN
LOUGH NEAGH
TYRONE
BELFAST
BANGOR
OMAGH DUNGANNON
PORTADOWN
LURGAN
ENNISKILLEN
ARMAGH
DOWN
DOWNPATRICK
FERMANAGH
ARMAGH
LEITRIM
MONAGHAN
NEWRY
IRISH SEA
CAVAN
LOUTH
N
MILES
0 —— 10

Contents

Preface   ix

Introduction   1

1. Overview   5

2. Explanations of the Northern Ireland Problem   29

3. The Effect of Religious Belief on the Conflict
   in Northern Ireland   57

4. 'Modernisation' and Northern Ireland   89

5. Is Religion Declining in Importance?   106

6. Towards a Sociological Analysis of Northern
   Ireland Society   118

Appendix: Study of a Community in Northern Ireland   127

Notes   141

Select Bibliography   147

Index   153

Preface

It has not been an easy task to write this book. Living in a society as turbulent as Northern Ireland's, and attempting to study it at the same time presents one with the major problem of achieving academic 'detachment'. There is always the danger of becoming too involved with the situations you are trying to analyse; of losing sight of the wood because you get lost in the trees.

In this situation I have relied heavily on the support and encouragement of a number of colleagues both within Northern Ireland and outside it. I am particularly grateful for the support and encouragement of Professors Jerry Suttles of the University of Chicago, Andrew Greeley, of NORC (National Opinion Research Centre), University of Chicago, and David Martin of the London School of Economics; they have all read and commented upon parts of the text. Professor T. Gannon, Loyola University, Chicago, provided me not only with considerable moral support but also a great deal of practical assistance while I was working in his department and starting to write the text.

I have benefited enormously from working closely with Dr John Whyte, Queen's University, Belfast, over a number of years and from discussions I have had with him and Mr John Darby of the New University of Ulster. I also owe a particular debt to my colleagues Professor Morton-Williams and Mr Joe McCormack of the Department of Social Anthropology and Sociology at NUU.

All of the above have contributed greatly to any merit the book may have; its defects are my own responsibility. Finally, I should like to thank the Committee for Social Research in Ireland and the Ford Foundation who provided the finance for the survey work reported on in the Appendix.

John Hickey   New University of Ulster
December 1983   Coleraine

Introduction

The State of Northern Ireland was born in violence and violence has been present below or above the surface of its everyday life ever since. There have been periods of internal quiet since 1920, and for twenty years after the last war it seemed as if the province's worst times were over. These were the years when the members of the Roman Catholic minority in particular were benefiting from the reforms introduced in education and welfare by the 1945 Labour government and applied, after due lapse of time, to Northern Ireland. The Roman Catholics shared in these benefits on the same footing as their Protestant neighbours and the former showed signs of concentrating their hopes and aspirations on developing a satisfying life-style within the context of the Six Counties and slowly abandoning the political ideal of a united Ireland.

To be sure, Roman Catholics were not yet, at this period, prepared to vote for the political party which represented the Protestant majority — the Unionist party with its policy of loyalty to Britain and maintenance of the *status quo*. To expect a change of that magnitude in one generation would be to expect too much. They also gave — as did their Protestant counterparts — only minimal and wavering support to a cross-sectarian party like the Northern Ireland Labour Party, whose policies put it more in line with the 'normal politics' of the remainder of the United Kingdom than any other political group in Northern Ireland.[1] But it is worthwhile to note that the NILP was making some impact in the late fifties and reached its peak of support in the early 1960s. The most significant indication of the mood of Roman Catholics during these years is to be found in the almost complete lack of support given to the campaign launched by the Irish Republican Army in 1956. This campaign ended, officially, in 1962 when the IRA finally admitted defeat due to lack of support among Northern Ireland's Roman Catholics and consequently began to develop a non-violent political strategy emphasising social reform throughout the whole of Ireland.[2] In this way there was at least a tacit recognition by the group that had traditionally represented the military expression of the national aspirations of Irish Catholics, based upon bitter experience, that some heed must be paid to the changing nature of the aspirations of Roman Catholics in the province.

Writing now, in 1981, while the most prolonged and vicious outbreak of violence in the history of the Northern Ireland State is still in progress, it is easy to see that the calm of the 1945-65 period and the hopes built upon it were superficial. The divisive forces were still there, though beneath the surface. It took a very few years in the mid-sixties to bring them back into view and the troubles which have plagued Northern Ireland since 1969 have turned the province into a major disaster area. The remainder of this work is an attempt to identify and explain one of the major and most deeply rooted causes of the present enduring conflict.

Before embarking on this, however, it is necessary to pause briefly to consider the problems facing the social scientist working in and on Northern Ireland. If you enter the situation from the outside — that is, you were not born and brought up in the province — as I did, then the first problem is one of self-adjustment. I do not mean by this simply personal adjustment to a culture different from that of mainland England and Wales. Nor am I speaking only of the further dimension of adjustment that needs to be made to the constant tension engendered by the violence and its concomitants. The latter include the day-by-day presence of heavily armed troops, the frequent stops at road-blocks, the constant searches in Belfast and other towns before entering stores and the melancholy presence of the battered centres of Belfast and Derry. What concerns me more than this is the adjustment needed not only to *live* in such an environment but also to study it.

The problem basically is one of dealing with a similarity which is not similar. The small towns in Northern Ireland look like small towns in many parts of England, particularly the north of England. The countryside resembles the landscapes of Yorkshire and the Lake District of Cumbria. Belfast is physically laid out like many industrial cities in the north of England; it is not a beautiful city but it loses nothing in comparison with Manchester, Leeds or Newcastle. External appearances would, then, indicate that the population to be studied has basically the same characteristics in terms of life-styles as those of any mixed rural-urban area of Britain.

It takes time to adjust to the realisation that this population is *not* the same. The intermittent violence of fifty years, plus the brutalities of the present outbreak, have not only resulted in widespread physical damage, injury and death. Damage has not only been done to life and property. Familiarity with the long, weary history of the province, living that history, has done violence to the norms of its citizens. It is possible now to think the unthinkable; to accept danger or death as a consequence simply of being a Roman Catholic or a Protestant; to accept savage retaliation − sectarian murders − as the way of keeping Northern Ireland's particular version of the 'balance of terror'. It could be summed up, I suppose, by saying that the members of Northern Ireland's society have learned to live with a degree of lawlessness which could not be imagined − let alone tolerated − in any other part of the United Kingdom.[3]

This is the final, and perhaps most difficult adjustment that the social scientist has to make in preparing himself mentally for the task of observation and analysis. To be exploring in familiar surroundings very unfamiliar values and norms puts an increased obligation on the student to understand the forces working below the surface which are affecting the whole life-styles of the people he is interested in. There is no real parallel he can make in British or American society; no reference points to turn to for comparison or enlightenment. The situation in Northern Ireland is unique and this means that an attempt to understand it must involve some analysis in depth of the people who comprise it. There have been a number of attempts to do this − to embark, if you like, on what is for the social scientist the 'beginning of wisdom'. Some of this work has been based upon the technique of participant observation favoured by social anthropologists. One of the best of these studies has been published: Rosemary Harris's study of a small village in the south-west of the province which has appeared under the title of *Prejudice and Tolerance in Ulster*. There has also been published, in book form, the excellent study by Elliott Leyton entitled *The One Blood*. But most of the work in this sphere remains unpublished and embedded in theses and dissertations produced by students, graduate and undergraduate. For a very good index of these see L. Blaxter *et al.*, *Irish Rural Society: A Selected Bibliography 1920-1972*. This bibliography is itself unpublished but is available in xeroxed form.

In terms of quantitative measurement — that is, employing the techniques of survey methodology — there is again an impressive amount of material available in unpublished form. The most significant work employing this method and setting the results in an historical framework is that of Richard Rose whose book *Governing without Consensus* is required reading for any serious student who is attempting to understand the present 'problem' in Northern Ireland. I have adopted survey methodology in my study of a small community in Northern Ireland and some of the results of that study are summarised in the Appendix to this book.

The fullest and most accessible bibliography of work on Northern Ireland is to be found in John Darby's book *Conflict in Northern Ireland*. Although the book was published in 1976, Darby has been able to include work completed as late as 1975. This bibliography will be supplemented and brought up to date by the index of research in progress currently being produced by Darby, Hepburn and Dodge and available through the Centre for the Study of Conflict at the New University of Ulster.

1
Overview

The substance of the work will deal with the questions which need to be addressed sociologically in order to attempt to isolate the factors which are the prime contributors to the present conflict. Attention, however, must be paid to the historical context which pervades the present situation and to the interpretations which have been so far advanced in terms of 'explanations' of the situation in Northern Ireland.

The purpose of this chapter will be, first of all, to summarise briefly the historical factors which have produced the present divided social situation. This will be followed by an identification of the sociological 'interpretations' of the conflict produced in the province and by an identification of the forces which seem to be operating in the present situation: modernisation and religion. Particular attention will be paid to religion because it is felt essential to demonstrate the importance of this aspect of daily life in a society where, although it is demonstrable that religion is the crucial 'divide', so many analyses attempt to downgrade its importance by allocating religion a purely symbolic significance. An attempt will be made to redress the balance in this respect.

It would obviously be inappropriate in this work to attempt even an outline of the history of Northern Ireland and its place in the history of Ireland as a whole. The interested reader will find this history more than adequately covered in a number of studies by prominent scholars.[1] We do need to look briefly, however, at the origin and nature of the province of Northern Ireland in its present form and to trace some of the developments since its foundation in 1920.

Ireland is divided into the four provinces of Ulster, Munster, Leinster and Connaught. The three areas of Munster,

Leinster and Connaught are now incorporated into the Republic of Ireland. Ulster consists of the nine counties of Fermanagh, Armagh, Tyrone, Londonderry, Antrim, Down, Donegal, Monaghan and Cavan. Of these nine counties of the historic province of Ulster, the first six were incorporated, by the Act of 1920, into the State of Northern Ireland and partitioned off not only from the remaining provinces of Ireland but from the three remaining counties of Ulster. Hence it is not strictly accurate, in an historical sense, to refer to the State of Northern Ireland as 'Ulster' because that State does not encompass the whole of the ancient province of Ulster. Nevertheless, the inhabitants of Northern Ireland, both Protestant and Roman Catholic, commonly refer to themselves as 'Ulstermen' in private conversation. In public, Roman Catholics tend either to use the phrase 'the Six Counties' — thereby keeping alive the traditional memories of an Ulster of nine counties — or the title 'Northern Ireland' for the State separate from and independent of the Republic of Ireland. Protestants tend almost exclusively to use in public the term 'Northern Ireland' for their own State. They are thus emphasising the union with Britain and their incorporation into the United Kingdom of Great Britain and Northern Ireland. For the sake of both historical and sociological accuracy, the term 'Northern Ireland' will be used throughout this work to describe the society under analysis.

This society, as a separate legal entity, came into existence in 1920. The occasion of its birth did not augur well for its future stability and prosperity. The current turmoil is evidence of the fact that the society of Northern Ireland is the reluctant inheritor of centuries of conflict within Ireland itself and between Ireland and what has now become Britain. The external conflict, between an Ireland which had settled, temporarily at least, its internal conflicts, and Britain, came to a head finally in the late nineteenth and early twentieth centuries.[2] During this period a sense of Irish nationalism developed among the majority of the inhabitants of Ireland and with it a desire for self-determination and independence from Britain.

Throughout the nineteenth century there were periods of

intense pressure on Britain to introduce Home Rule for Ireland. This pressure reached its peak in the last three decades of the century but political divisions within Britain made it inexpedient for that country to grant the reforms demanded.[3] Thus, at the close of the nineteenth century, Britain had made a declaration of intent — in Gladstone's famous phrase, the mission of his Liberal government was to pacify Ireland, with implications that this 'pacification' meant Home Rule — but had not been able, or willing, to implement it. The efforts of their own politicians, plus the public statements of the British government, had convinced the politically aware of the four provinces that Home Rule for Ireland was immediately achievable.

Why then the delay? For the inhabitants of Munster, Leinster and Connaught, the delay was the result of British 'perfidy'. The government at Westminster had no real intention of fulfilling the aspirations of the 'Irish people' and were only playing for time. Once the time had been adequately used, the British would simply reinstate themselves in their position as the ruling caste who were ultimately aimed at exploiting a subject people. The British political parties viewed that delay in a very different light. Their problem was, basically, who should control the destiny of a highly complex society with a long imperialistic tradition and an industrial structure which needed and demanded reform. Prestige abroad and the national security that that involved were of paramount concern. The question of the four provinces of Ireland was not of primary importance. It became important only when it intervened in more pressing problems of state, and when Irish members of the Westminster Parliament were able to exert a powerful influence upon the party in government.

This situation was demonstrated in the first decade of the twentieth century. The Liberal government of 1906 was able to survive without the support of Irish members of Parliament and therefore could concentrate its efforts upon the social reforms which were of pressing need in Britain's industrialised society. Home Rule for Ireland took second place to legislation aimed at improving the living conditions of the vast mass of Britain's industrial workers. Improvement of the

style of life of the majority of the citizens of what was, by
that date, a highly complex urbanised, industrial society
took priority over the demands of a relatively small, pre-
dominantly rural population for self-determination. So,
between 1906 and 1910, the Liberal government, mainly
through the activities of Lloyd George, began a programme
of social welfare legislation which was to culminate, almost
forty years later, in the 'Welfare State' introduced by the
first post-war Labour government.

In 1910, however, at the end of their first four-year period
of government the Liberals lost their overall majority at
Westminster and the Irish members of Parliament held the
balance of power. The granting of Home Rule for Ireland
now became imminent. The delay already referred to,
however, had resulted within Ireland in the growth of
patriots who aimed at achieving power by force or other
non-constitutional means. Chief among these groups were
the Irish Republican Brotherhood, who had developed a
strong following amongst Irish-Americans and who had
grown in strength and influence throughout the second
half of the nineteenth century, and Sinn Féin. The latter
group, which was to become the most powerful and
important, was established much later by Arthur Griffith
at a meeting in Dublin in 1905.

On a different level, the last part of the nineteenth century and the beginning of the twentieth century saw a great
increase in interest in things Irish, an interest which em-
braced language, literature, customs and traditions which
were judged to have their roots in Ireland. This was accompanied by a 'Renaissance' in Anglo-Irish literature and the
period saw the emergence of poets, dramatists and novelists
whose work is identified with Ireland and who have become
internationally known and honoured. Though much of this
latter work was written in English and is the product of the
mingling of both British and Irish influences, the whole
movement in general helped to strengthen the development
of Irish national sentiment both in Ireland itself and abroad.

What, however, of the majority of the inhabitants of that
fourth province of Ireland — Ulster? How did they use the
delay?[4] The Unionists of the North, Protestant by religion

and British by tradition, were strongly opposed to Home Rule for Ireland and wanted to keep the close link with the British monarchy and the imperial Parliament at Westminster. They had made these sentiments very clear during the closing decades of the nineteenth century and had received substantial encouragement and support from the Conservative Party both within Parliament and outside it. They used the delay as one might have expected — to organise themselves to repel any attempt made to push them into a united Ireland independent of Britain. This they had done so effectively that, by the time the Home Rule Bill came before Parliament in 1912, the Northern Ireland Unionists had already drafted a constitution which provided for a Provisional Government of Ulster. More significantly, perhaps, they had also raised a volunteer army which was pledged to defend the 'liberties of Protestants'.[5] At the same time, in a very successful effort to exploit the symbolic aspects of their cause and the emotions it aroused, they launched, in 1912, a campaign to collect pledges to a 'Solemn League and Covenant' which bound subscribers to use 'all means which may be found necessary to defeat the present conspiracy to set up a Home Rule Parliament in Ireland. And in the event of such a Parliament being forced upon us we further solemnly and mutually pledge ourselves to refuse to recognise its authority.'[6] Almost half a million citizens signed this pledge, some of them in their own blood.

The effect of this 'Solemn League and Covenant' upon the spirit and morale of Ulster Protestants was momentous and enduring. There are still a number of Protestants in Northern Ireland who will describe themselves as 'Covenanters', and an even greater number who will claim, with pride, that their parents and grandparents were among those who put their signatures to the document. The Covenant was at once a symbol of internal solidarity and common interest and of defiance of those external forces that would make the Protestant Unionist give up his loyalty to the Crown, accept an alien rule and lose his homeland. In the face of hostility of this breadth and level of intensity, the British government was uncertain what tactics to adopt to carry through its planned measure of Home Rule for Ireland. The government was not in a strong position. All-out resistance by Ulster Unionists was not the only problem it had to deal with. The Conservative party at Westminster was strongly in sympathy with the Unionists and certain to give the latter a great deal of support. It would be politically and ideologically impossible for Liberals and Conservatives to unite on the issue and agree a common policy. There was, furthermore, the very real possibility that the British troops stationed in Ireland could not be relied upon to put down by force a Protestant insurrection. A mutiny in the Army was a prospect no government could face with equanimity. While the British government was being tentative and uncertain, the Protestants of Ulster continued their preparations. Successful gun-running operations were completed — notably those at Bangor and Larne in 1914 — and the citizen volunteer army, now styled the Ulster Volunteer Force, was growing in size and strength.[7] By 1914 the militant Ulster Unionists were confident that they had the will and the means to resist forcible incorporation into an independent Ireland. Home Rule could be and would be opposed by all means necessary — and opposed successfully.

Open war in Ulster was averted by the outbreak of the First World War in 1914. During the period of that war, 1914-1918, events in the south of Ireland, particularly the Dublin Easter Rising of 1916, convinced the British government, if further evidence was indeed necessary for such conviction, that meeting the demands of Irish nationalists could only be postponed until after the international conflict ceased. When that happened, some form of Home Rule had to be granted to Ireland. A solution to the 'problem' of Ireland had to be found, but that solution had to take into account the demands and aspirations of the Protestants of Ulster. There could be no forcible unification of the four provinces of Ireland into one stable and sovereign nation. There was a pressing need for 'Home Rule for Ireland,' but what sort of 'Home Rule' and for what parts of Ireland?

The answer produced by the British Parliament was embodied in the Government of Ireland Act 1920. This legislation provided for two Parliaments in Ireland, one in the North and one in the South; there was also to be a Council of

Ireland to link both of these bodies. (The idea of a Council of Ireland was to re-emerge in 1974 and to contribute to the significant events of that year in Northern Ireland. This will be referred to later in the text.) The Parliament in the South was, of course, to be located in Dublin; the Parliament in the North came to be established just outside Belfast, at Stormont. This solution was not able to operate in full. Political turbulence and guerilla warfare continued in the South of Ireland and in 1921 Britain was obliged to grant the Irish Free State, as it became known, what was effectively Dominion status. The North, however, was given the right to stay out of this new State and its position and integrity were protected. Hence, the State of Northern Ireland came into being. Its links with the British Crown and its Parliament in Westminster were guaranteed and its jurisdiction was restricted to the internal affairs of six of the counties of Ulster — Fermanagh, Armagh, Tyrone, Londonderry, Antrim and Down. Foreign policy was reserved to Westminster and the British Parliament retained ultimate sovereignty over Northern Ireland. Nevertheless, the Northern Ireland State existed. It was the bulwark the Protestants of Ulster needed against incorporation into a united Ireland and constituted an assurance that their links with Britain would not be forcibly severed.

Nationalist Roman Catholic feelings in the South were affronted by the creation of this new, small State. They optimistically regarded the settlement as being essentially of a temporary nature and aimed at assuaging Protestant hostility in the North and avoiding direct and violent conflict. Hopes were aroused that a Boundary Commission, set up to examine the extent to which the whole of the Six Counties should remain in Northern Ireland, would result in a whittling away of the physical size of the new State to the point where it became no longer viable as an independent entity. Protestant, Unionist opinion was that they had only been granted what was theirs as of right. Some amongst them would have preferred total integration into the governmental structure of mainland Britain rather than the creation of their own Parliament. Others would have wished to have all nine counties of Ulster incorporated into the new State. All, however, agreed that control of the six-county region was the minimum they were entitled to and that no part of that territory would be given up. 'Not an inch' became, and still remains, a slogan to arouse strong fervour amongs Northern Protestants. This sentiment, plus others like 'No surrender', may be found painted on the walls of Protestant areas of towns in Northern Ireland. Sometimes such slogans are accompanied by murals depicting William of Orange's victory at the battle of the Boyne in 1690. History is not enshrined in text books in Northern Ireland. As in the Irish Republic it is a powerful motivator of contemporary action.

The basic lines for future political conflict were thus laid down. Nationalistic sentiment in the South, aimed at incorporating Northern Ireland into a united Ireland ruled from Dublin, has been met by a determination in the North to resist such a fate and to retain intact what was fought for and achieved in the first two decades of this century — a Northern Ireland independent of the South and linked with Britain. That Northern Ireland *has* remained intact. In 1925 the Irish Free State acknowledged the fact that the Boundary Commission was *not* going to encroach upon the frontier laid down in 1920; the physical size of Northern Ireland was to remain that encompassed by the six counties. The Dublin government grudgingly acknowledged the situation and accepted payments from the British government in return for their guarantee of the territorial integrity of Northern Ireland. But nationalist sentiment, aimed at achieving a totally united Ireland, regardless of the wishes of the Protestant population of the North, was not appeased. Irish politicians in the South were under constant pressure to remove the frontier in the North and place the whole of the island under one government located in Dublin. As a result, the Irish Constitution, promulgated in 1937, effectively abrogated the agreement of 1925 and laid sovereign claim to the six counties of Northern Ireland. They — the counties — were to be regarded as an area of Ireland temporarily and illegally outside the control of the Dublin government. The majority of the inhabitants of those counties — the Protestants — were not consulted when that clause was inserted into the Irish Constitution. Their reactions to this further threat to their integrity can be imagined. It can also be measured by the degree of violent conflict which has characterised the State of Northern Ireland and its relationship with its southern neighbour for the last sixty years.[8]

It is necessary, now, to look briefly at the demographic and social structure of Northern Ireland. At the time of writing the total population is approximately one and a half million people, that is, at least one third of the total population of the whole island of Ireland. Of this population of Northern Ireland, approximately one third are Roman Catholics and the remaining two thirds are Protestants.[9] The Roman Catholics, in religious terms, are, of course, one coherent and relatively cohesive group. The term 'Protestant', on the other hand, covers membership in a variety of Churches and denominations. The two largest Protestant groups are the Presbyterian and the Church of Ireland. Between them they account for rather more than 80 per cent of the total Protestant population of Northern Ireland, with the Presbyterians being slightly more numerous than the members of the Church of Ireland. The other groupings are much smaller in membership. The Methodists follow the Church of Ireland in numerical size but constitute only 20 per cent of the latter's membership. The next largest group is the Baptist Church and the remaining Protestant population is spread over half-a-dozen denominations, including the Reverend Ian Paisley's Free Presbyterians.[10]

Protestants and Roman Catholics are not divided into two clearly demarcated geographical enclaves. It is customary to refer to Protestants as living east of the River Bann and Roman Catholics as living to the west of the Bann (see map). This generalisation, while true of the *majority* of each religious group, hides a much more complex picture. Protestants and Roman Catholics are scattered throughout the entire province with the former heavily concentrated in the counties of Antrim and Down and the city of Belfast and the latter in the border area of counties Fermanagh and Armagh and in the counties of Tyrone and Londonderry. But there are substantial Protestant populations in all of these counties and sizeable Roman Catholic groups in Belfast, Antrim and Down.[11] Outside of the cities of Belfast and

Derry, which have to be treated as special cases, relationships between the two groups tend to vary according to the proximity of the towns and villages to the border, where there is sustained and violent conflict, and the religious make-up of the population. Generally speaking, the larger the majority one religious group has over the other, the less likelihood there is of violence. No part of the province has completely escaped the violence of the present strife but the factors of the relative size of each group to the other does seem to affect the *level* of that violence.[12] This may be due to the fact that the fewer Roman Catholics there are in relation to Protestants (and vice versa), the less 'visible' they are, and the less of a threat they constitute to the integrity and life-style of the larger group.[13]

The urban areas of Derry and Belfast are different and special cases. Apart from the battle-zones along the border with the Irish Republic, most of the violence in the present conflict has been concentrated in these two cities. This is both cause of and result from the demographic structure of both places. Both are ghettoised, with Protestants and Roman Catholics able to live out most of their daily lives within their 'own' territories, which are clearly marked-off from each other. Both, also, have historical traditions which make violence between Protestant and Roman Catholic inhabitants endemic. Derry, with its population of approximately 56,000, occupies a unique symbolic position within the historical and mythological traditions of both religious groups. The Roman Catholics see it as an ancient city and port which has played a major role in long centuries of the history and development of Irish culture. They resent the fact that its original name was changed by English merchants in the seventeenth century to Londonderry and refuse to refer to the city as other than 'Derry'. (Indeed, it is claimed that one can identify a Roman Catholic or a Protestant by whether he or she uses the name Derry or Londonderry, though in my experience, at least, both religious groups commonly use the shorter version, Derry.)[14]

There is also great resentment among the Roman Catholic inhabitants about what they regard as the deliberate neglect, on the part of the Stormont government, of the economic

welfare of what is the largest centre of population west of
the Bann. Because Roman Catholics constitute a majority of
the population of Derry, this 'neglect' is put down to
religious bias on the part of the Protestant-controlled
Northern Ireland government. This resentment was re-fuelled
in the mid 1960s when a government decision was made to
locate Northern Ireland's new university, the New University
of Ulster, at Coleraine — a Protestant-dominated town just
east of the Bann — rather than at Derry, where a university
college already existed.

To Protestants, Derry is famous in *their* history for the
events of 1688-89. In 1688 the Protestant people of Derry,
who occupied the old, walled city of that time, closed the
gates and prepared to resist the advancing armies of the
Roman Catholic king, James II. They held out successfully
under siege for a considerable period of time until they were
relieved by the forces of the Protestant king, William of
Orange. That victory has become a central feature of
Protestant mythology.[15] It is still celebrated in August
every year when the Protestant organisation, the Apprentice
Boys, march around the old part of the city, symbolically
claiming it as their own.

The city of Belfast is by far the largest centre of population
in Northern Ireland. Its inhabitants total around 560,000,
i.e. approximately 36 per cent of the total population of the
province. Of the total inhabitants of Belfast, 26 per cent are
Roman Catholic — a minority, but a substantial one consider-
ing the actual number of people who comprise it. The 'visibility' of this Roman Catholic group is increased by the fact
that it is highly ghettoised. More than 80 per cent of the
Roman Catholic community reside in two adjacent areas
lying to the west of the River Lagan which runs through the
city. These areas, known commonly as the 'Falls' and the
'Ardoyne', consist largely of groups of streets of small houses
with a number of public housing estates located among them.
The total area is not large but is very densely populated by
people who have developed a strong sense of their own
identity, based upon common religious affiliation.[16]

The questions of this 'identity', its religious base and
the attitudes developed thereon to political ideology and the

nature of the State will be addressed later in this work.[17] The point to be made here is the fact of the existence of a numerically large, cohesive minority group within a closely-knit urban population, and the social factors which develop from this situation. To the majority of the population of Belfast it is not only apparent that Roman Catholics exist there but that they exist *separately*. The Roman Catholic section of Belfast constitutes a ghetto in the true sense of the word. Though it comprises a minority of the population of the city, the Roman Catholic group is large enough to support its own 'different' life-style. It can provide not only a range of day-to-day contacts sufficient to satisfy the needs of its inhabitants but also enough recreational facilities to make it unnecessary to move outside the area to find relief and relaxation.[18] More significantly, perhaps, it is able, through the structures set up and largely controlled by the clergy, to provide not only its own churches but also a school system large enough to cater for all the children of school age. It has, furthermore, two Colleges of Education of its own to provide teachers for these schools. It is, in fact, a city within a city. It is a ghetto; not simply physically segregated from the rest of Belfast but, in a sense, proclaiming its own separate and independent existence from the rest of the urban community of which it is notionally a part. To the remainder of the citizens of Belfast, the Roman Catholic area has a life and life-style of its own which can exist separately from and independently of them and to which they are not welcome to enter. In such a situation, mutual fear, suspicion and hostility naturally develop, and violence is never far from the surface.[19]

The question may be asked, at this point, as to how this situation came about in Belfast. The historical background to the birth of Northern Ireland State has been briefly touched upon already. In the case of Belfast, a more considered account of the development of the relationships between the two religious groups in the city is indicated.

From the early seventeenth century, Belfast was essentially a Protestant town. There had always been a small Roman Catholic minority there but their absolute numbers and proportion of the total population of the town had never been sufficient to challenge the authority and integrity of the life-style of the Protestant majority. This had enabled the latter to develop not only tolerant but positively sympathetic attitudes towards their Roman Catholic fellow townsfolk. The distrust and hostility between Protestant and Roman Catholic, which is so characteristic of Belfast now, did not exist then in the early years of its development as a town. It is worth noting, however, that this peaceful relationship between the two groups was not, even in the time-scale commonly associated with Irish cultural memories, a fleeting phenomenon. It actually lasted until the end of the eighteenth century. Protestants, for example, made substantial contributions to the building of the first Roman Catholic church, St Mary's in Chapel Lane, due to be opened in the town in May 1784. When that opening took place, the Volunteers, an exclusively Protestant organisation, added to the pomp and circumstance of the occasion, as the following quotation shows:

> On Sunday last the Belfast First Company and Belfast Volunteer Company paraded in full dress and marched to mass, where a sermon was preached by the Rev. Mr O'Donnell, and a handsome collection made to aid in defraying the expense of erecting the new mass-house. Great numbers of other Protestant inhabitants also attended.[20]

This was not the only demonstration, during that period, of Protestant support and sympathy for their Roman Catholic fellow townsfolk. In the late eighteenth century a body named the Catholic Convention had come into existence in Ireland. It claimed full political rights for Roman Catholics throughout the British Isles. In 1793 the Catholic Convention decided to send a group of delegates to London as part of their political campaign for equal rights. The delegation passed through Belfast on their way to England and the townspeople took the opportunity to express their support by turning out to cheer the delegates on their way and wish them success in their venture.[21]

These two examples are cited to demonstrate the mutual toleration and support which existed between the two religious groups, at least up until the end of the eighteenth century. Why then, did the situation change and degenerate into the now more familiar scene of hostility, suspicion and mistrust? The answer to this question must be looked for in the working out of economic and social factors in the nineteenth century. Belfast shared with mainland Britain the effects of the rapid growth of industrialisation and urban development in the nineteenth century. The shipbuilding industry grew rapidly during this period as did the linen and textile mills and factories in the city. Inevitably, these developments were accompanied by a very substantial and accelerated growth in the population of the town, and this, to quote J. C. Beckett, 'brought with it profound and disturbing effects on the social and political life of the town, effects that are not yet exhausted more than a hundred years later' (1967, p. 187).

As Beckett points out, it was not simply the fact that this growth took place so rapidly which was to prove so significant a factor in the relationships between the religious groups in the town. Rather it was the character of the growth which was to have the most disturbing effects upon religious harmony in Belfast. There was a high proportion of Roman Catholics among the thousands of people who moved into Belfast, attracted by the prospect of employment and regular wages. This proportion grew so large that by the middle of the nineteenth century Roman Catholics constituted more than one third of the total population of Belfast and were concentrated largely in the western part of the town. By 1851, then, the foundations of the present Roman Catholic ghetto in Belfast were firmly established.

The Protestant residents were deeply disturbed by this radical and rapid change in the denominational balance of the town. They had been able to be tolerant and sympathetic to Roman Catholics when the latter constituted only an insignificant proportion of the total population. Now, however, they were confronted with a strong and compact group of people of the 'other' religion who could pose a real threat to their control of the town. It was, furthermore, not only the physical size of the group which worried the Protestants. Irish Roman Catholics, especially since the era

of Daniel O'Connell, had shown themselves quick to learn
how to exert influence through political organisations — a
learning they were to put to a very good use in the big
cities in the United States later on in the nineteenth and
twentieth centuries — and they were, potentially, very
dangerous to those well-established groups who held power
in Belfast. A. C. Hepburn quotes a statement which helps
to demonstrate this point. It was made in 1857 by one
Bernard Hughes who delivered himself of the opinion that
'This town is governed by Protestants, but the bone and
sinew of the town is Roman Catholic. What I mean by
this is that this is a Roman Catholic town.'[22] The confidence
which lay behind Hughes's statement — he was the sole
Roman Catholic representative on the Belfast City Council
at the time — helped only to fuel the fires of Protestant fears
that their town was to be taken from them and did nothing
to improve relationships between Protestants and Roman
Catholics in Belfast at that time.

The Protestant workers were, as one would expect, the
first group to develop suspicion and hostility towards the
incoming Roman Catholics. The latter competed directly
with them for employment and housing and mutual anti-
pathy between the two groups erupted into violence on a
number of occasions. 'Middle-class' and 'upper-class'
Protestants did not become involved in physical violence
but they were determined, none the less, to retain control
of civic affairs.

In some respects, what happened in Belfast in this connection followed a classic pattern in terms of the urban
conflict which results from an influx of 'alien' people. The
immigration of the Irish Roman Catholic workers into the
industrial cities of mainland Britain, for example, also often
provoked conflict and violence with the indigenous workers
and brought hostility from the groups which controlled civic
affairs.[23] The same pattern can also be seen in the movements
of ethnic groups into the cities of the United States. It is
characteristic of urban development in the nineteenth and
twentieth centuries that wherever a group of people of
substantial size and distinctive characteristics attempted to
establish themselves within a 'host' population of differing

characteristics, some degree of hostility and, sometimes, violence resulted. In most cases the period of conflict was relatively short-lived, accommodation was reached between the two sides and mutual tolerance leading to acceptance developed. One of the distinctive features of the urban development of Belfast is that this pattern was *not* followed. Conflict and violence between Protestants and Roman Catholics has been characteristic of the city from the middle of the nineteenth century until today. If we take the period from 1850 to the formation of the Northern Ireland State in 1920 we can see plenty of evidence of this turmoil. Legislation was enacted in order to try at least to reduce the likelihood of violence — examples of this are the Party Processions Act of 1850, the Party Emblems Act of 1860 and a by-law prohibiting sectarian language — but it did not prove to be very effective.[24] There was sectarian rioting in the town in 1857, 1864, 1872, 1893, 1898, and 1912 — a dreary catalogue bearing witness to the inability of Protestants and Roman Catholics to live peacefully with each other.

It should now be apparent that when the State of Northern Ireland was established in 1920 it inherited problems which did not augur well for its future prosperity and stability. This is not the point at which to reflect at length on the nature of the link between the state, as an institution of government, and the society whose wishes it is meant to express and whose actions it is designed to control. Such a project would be worth while, but well beyond the scope of this book. We are concerned, primarily, with the situation of Northern Ireland society now, and not with the problem of whether 'Northern Ireland' should have existed in the first place. Northern Ireland exists and must be dealt with as an empirical reality. We should, however, make a distinction between the term 'state' and the term 'society' in order to shift the focus of the discussion into a sociological framework. In this context, 'society' is the group of people living within geographically determined boundaries and developing institutions — religious, economic, political and educational — which reflect a commonly agreed and accepted pattern of life, and 'state' is the system of government which reflects the wishes and aspirations of the people of the society whose destiny it is meant to direct.

The 'State' of Northern Ireland was set up, by agreement between external powers and a proportion of its own population, to direct, through its governmental and bureaucratic structures, the destinies of a society which had not reached common agreement upon the institutions mentioned above. It not only inherited a tradition of conflict and hostility but was faced, from the outset, with the problem of governing a society where the root causes of that conflict and violence were built into its geographic, demographic and institutional structures. The 'society' consisted of two groups of people divided by the consciousness of different historical and religious traditions and accustomed to confronting each other across a divide created by those traditions. Given this situation, it is surprising that the society of Northern Ireland has been as stable as it has, prior to the present long outbreak of violence.

Northern Ireland has not, of course, been 'stable' in comparison to the remainder of the United Kingdom. In 1921-22, the years immediately following its establishment, violence reached a peak which was not matched until almost fifty years later. In 1922 alone two hundred and thirty-two people were killed in outbreaks of sectarian violence: street battles occurred which went beyond the limits of 'riots' and verged on civil war. After 1922 a period of comparative calm ensued, perhaps induced by fear and exhaustion following the bloodshed of that year. This period lasted approximately ten years and during it the Northern Ireland State began to establish its governmental structures. The Civil Service bureaucracy was set up, local government bodies established and the police force — the Royal Ulster Constabulary — formed. During this period, also, the formal education system was laid down, amid much dispute and contention between Protestants and Roman Catholics, and the basis formed for the present system which, up to and including high school level, is segregated on religious grounds.[25]

From 1932 to 1935 there were again outbreaks of violence between the two religious groups and further Protestant fears were aroused in 1937 by the promulgation of the new Constitution for the Irish Republic. As has been noted already, this Constitution contained within it a claim of sovereignty over the whole island of Ireland, including the six counties of Northern Ireland. Furthermore, the document gave the Roman Catholic Church a guaranteed 'special position' within the Irish Republic. The turbulence of the thirties took place in a context of economic depression; during that period the unemployment rate in Northern Ireland never dropped below 25 per cent.

The Second World War of 1939-1945 saw a further period of comparative calm within Northern Ireland and the war years were succeeded by almost two decades during which violence and hostility at last seemed to be giving way to peace and stability. The war years saw an economic boom in Northern Ireland and this was followed by the implementation of legislation passed in Westminster, designed to promote improvements in social conditions. This legislation included the establishment of a Housing Trust, in 1945, aimed at improving the quality and supply of houses in Northern Ireland, and the beginning of a long-term industrial development policy. The Acts aimed at laying the foundations of the so-called 'Welfare State' in Britain were also extended to Northern Ireland. These included the 1947 Education Act, which established compulsory and free secondary education for those who could demonstrate their academic ability to benefit from it, and the National Assistance and Health Services Acts of 1948. After the Irish Republic left the British Commonwealth, in 1949, the Ireland Act guaranteed Northern Ireland's position within the United Kingdom.

All in all, the signs were promising for political stability and social advancement. It was a period of re-building and optimism and this optimism seemed to be confirmed by the failure of the advocates of violence to gain much encouragement from the population. As has been noted earlier, the Irish Republican Army, operating in Northern Ireland, began a guerilla campaign in 1956 but this petered out finally in 1962 without making much impact upon society. The leaders of the IRA conceded that their lack of success was due to the fact that they were able to gain little support from the Roman Catholic population in Northern Ireland. As a result, a decision was made by the IRA leadership to concentrate their efforts on more 'normal' political activity and to abandon violence as a means of achieving their aims.

Optimism ended in the sixties when violence and conflict once again came to dominate Northern Ireland society. No attempt will be made at this point to give a full detailed account of the events which began the present outbreak or which have characterised the period from 1969 to 1981. Such accounts are available from other sources. Analyses of the significance of some of these events for the social structure of Northern Ireland will appear at later stages in this work. A brief narrative is necessary, however, to 'set the scene'.

In 1964 a Campaign for Social Justice began in Northern Ireland. The 'Social Justice' demanded included equal rights for Roman Catholics in terms of voting, particularly in local government elections where eligibility for the vote depended on ownership or occupation of property rather than upon the principle of one man one vote. Roman Catholics were also seeking equal opportunities in employment — where it was felt certain employers discriminated in favour of Protestants — and fair treatment in the allocation of public housing where, it was felt, certain local government authorities discriminated in favour of Protestants. The campaign was accompanied by disturbances in Belfast during elections. In 1965 there was an historically significant meeting at Stormont between Prime Minister O'Neill of Northern Ireland and Prime Minister Lemass of the Irish Republic. This was the first public meeting between Prime Ministers of North and South since the formation of the State of Northern Ireland and the event deeply disturbed some sections of the Protestant population who suspected it as the start of a process aimed at the eventual unification of Ireland and the disappearance of Northern Ireland as an independent entity.

1966 saw the fiftieth anniversary of the 1916 Easter Rising in Dublin. Suspecting a re-emergence of the IRA and the launching of a further campaign of violence to 'celebrate' the anniversary, a group of Protestant militants formed an organisation called the Ulster Volunteer Force, dedicated to the defeat and destruction of the IRA. The UVF were responsible for a number of murders in Belfast in 1966 and several of its members were convicted and jailed.

Tension and hostility continued to mount as 1966 drew to a close, but probably the most significant event in bringing about the start of the present conflict was to occur in 1967. In that year the Northern Ireland Civil Rights Association (NICRA) was formed and drew up a programme aimed at achieving complete equality in all aspects of civil rights for Roman Catholics. The campaign in support of the programme was taken on to the streets in 1968 and a combination of the classic tactics used in Northern Ireland to promote or celebrate causes and those learnt from the Civil Rights movement in the United States was used by its leaders. The 'classic tactics' were those of marches and the imports included songs and sit-ins. The Civil Rights marches began in August 1968 and continued, at intervals, until December. The first marches went off relatively peacefully but serious violence occurred in October as the result of a march to Derry. The government had, in fact, banned this march because they feared trouble between Protestants and Roman Catholics in a place like Derry where, as has been noted, conflict between the two religious groups was always near the surface. In spite of the ban, the march went ahead and police charged the marchers in an attempt to disperse them. This provoked serious rioting which continued throughout the night of 5 October.

Certain reforms were announced by the government in response to the pressure from the Civil Rights campaigners but Protestant hostility was rising and in November a group led by the Reverend Ian Paisley occupied Armagh, a town in the south of the province, and forced a Civil Rights march to be diverted. An increasing number of Protestants were coming to identify the Civil Rights campaign with the old Roman Catholic demand for unification with the Irish Republic and were convinced that the IRA were controlling the movement. Any concessions, then, granted to NICRA were seen as threats to Protestant control over Northern Ireland and, hence, as a danger to the existence of the State itself. Dismayed both by this hostile reaction and by the violence which had attended its campaign, the Northern

Ireland Civil Rights Association in December announced a
'truce' and declared that no further marches or demonstrations
would be held.

At this stage a new organisation appeared on the scene.
This was a group calling itself the 'People's Democracy'
and formed largely of students from Queen's University,
Belfast.[26] People's Democracy operated independently of
NICRA and announced that they would hold a march across
Northern Ireland from Belfast to Derry in January 1969.
The march took place, in spite of pressure from various
groups, including NICRA, to stop it, and was attacked by
Protestant loyalists at Burntollet, not far from Derry. A
further PD march later that same month in Newry provoked
further rioting. The conflict was beginning to gather momen-
tum. The following months saw a general election to the
Northern Ireland Parliament and the fall of the Unionist
Prime Minister, O'Neill. He resigned following pressure from
members of his own party who were dissatisfied with his
policies towards the civil rights campaigners and who thought
he was granting too many concessions to the minority group.

August 1969 is generally regarded as the crucial date in
the start of the present 'troubles' in Northern Ireland. On the
12th of that month an Apprentice Boys march in Derry —
commemorating the anniversary of the lifting of the siege —
was attacked. Police intervened to protect the marchers and
then attempted to storm the Bogside, one of the major
Roman Catholic areas in Derry. Rioting followed which
lasted all night and into the next day. Unlike previous outbreaks, which had been localised, this rioting spread during
the 13th and 14th August to various other areas in Northern
Ireland. The outbreak in Belfast was particularly vicious and
resulted in the deaths of four men and a boy. Units of the
British Army were drafted into Belfast to attempt to restore
some sort of order between the two groups and a so-called
'peace line' was established at the edge of the Falls ghetto
to separate it from the Protestant Shankill area. The presence
of the troops was supposed to be a temporary measure until
calm was restored. They are still there, in force, twelve years
later.

As was indicated earlier, the events of those twelve years

will not be catalogued here. There are certain 'highlights', however, which should be mentioned before this section of the work is brought to a close. In January 1970, at a meeting of Sinn Féin, (the political wing of the IRA) in Dublin, there was a major disagreement over the policy which should be applied in Northern Ireland. The dispute centred upon the question of whether or not violence should be used to protect the Roman Catholic population in Belfast and to carry the war into the 'enemy' camp. Those advocating physical force as a policy finally walked out of the meeting. This was the start of the formation of the 'Provisional' IRA and a split in the movement itself between them and the remainder who became known as the 'Official' IRA. The Provisional IRA are conducting the campaign of physical force in Northern Ireland. Their counterpart among Protestants, though a much smaller group, would be the UVF mentioned earlier.

In the following years, intermittent rioting has occurred, mainly in Belfast and Derry, and 'sectarian assassinations' — murders of members of each religious group by the other — have taken place all over Northern Ireland. There have been some peaks of activity. In August 1971, for example, following the introduction of internment by the Northern Ireland government and the arrest of some 300 people, there was widespread violence and arson. Two hundred and forty houses were burned down and eleven people killed in one day. But violence and tension have been constant and widespread throughout the whole of Northern Ireland since 1969 with the news bulletins each day adding to the dreary record of 'incidents'. In an attempt to tighten control and enforce 'law and order' the British government used its power under the 1920 Act to suspend the Northern Ireland Parliament in March 1972 and introduce direct rule from Westminster. The State of Northern Ireland thus lost its autonomy and self-direction. In July 1973 the Northern Ireland Constitution Act became law and Stormont was abolished. Since that time various constitutional 'experiments' have been tried and conferences held in order to try to find some form of government *for* Northern Ireland *in* Northern Ireland which would be acceptable to the whole society and able to operate effectively.

None of these experiments have been successful and Northern Ireland continues to be ruled directly from Westminster.

The death toll from the conflict in Northern Ireland continues to rise steadily. There have now been more than 2,000 people killed since 1969, civilians and members of the security forces. The worst year so far has been 1972, an ironic fiftieth anniversary of the previous worst year of 1922. The bloodshed of 1922, which brought 232 deaths, was followed by a period of relative calm. The bloodshed of 1972, which brought 468 deaths (322 civilians and 146 members of the security forces), served only to prolong the violence into the new decade.

The remainder of this work will be an attempt to analyse some of the major factors which are contributing to the turbulence which afflicts the society of Northern Ireland and to the length of the present outbreak of violence. Particular attention will be paid to the roles that religion and the content of religious belief are playing in the situation. Before this, however, some account will be taken of a number of the all-embracing 'explanations' of the Northern Ireland problem which have been advanced. These will include the 'politico-cultural' explanations which see the social conflict in terms of a struggle between two alien 'cultures'. In these categories we have the school of thought which sees the struggle in straightforward political terms as a bitter fight between Irish nationalism and British loyalist Unionism. Alternatively, the political contest may be viewed as a struggle by Irish Republicanism to rid itself of the oppressive yoke of British imperialism. The advocates of the 'cultural' explanation will speak in terms of two groups with radically different 'cultures' unable to co-exist within the same society.

These arguments will be discussed in the next chapter. At the same time the new 'sociological' analysis and interpretation which has recently been advanced, based on elements derived from a Marxist school of thought, will be considered at some length. This is a persuasive interpretation but it contains, in my view, certain flaws which detract substantially from its usefulness as an overall explanation of a very complex problem. The part played by religion in the Northern Ireland problem will be discussed at stages throughout the remainder of the book. Finally, attention will be paid to the effect that the process of 'modernisation' is having on the situation and a sociological model will be proposed to assist in understanding the changing nature of the society of Northern Ireland.

2
Explanations of the Northern Ireland Problem

Many attempts have been made during the last twenty-five years to analyse and explain the situation in the society of Northern Ireland which is giving rise to the physical conflict here. These attempts have increased in number, though not necessarily always in depth and quality, since the violence was resumed here more than a decade and a half ago. The major analyses and explanations have been categorised by Darby (1976) and Whyte (1971) and the reader is recommended to both these sources as valuable surveys of the scholarly work which has been applied to further understanding of the complexities of the Northern Ireland 'problem'. A number of sociological models have been applied, involving the use of major concepts like 'race', 'caste', 'ethnicity' and 'cultural assimilation', with varying degrees of success; the explanatory power of these concepts depends a great deal upon the degree of precision with which they are defined and the extent to which the authors using them are familiar with the society they are discussing. In this respect the application of models, developed to analyse the structures of quite different societies, to Northern Ireland, is not often particularly helpful without considerable refinement. To use, for example, an unmodified 'race relations' model imported from the United States, substituting Protestants for Whites and Roman Catholics for Blacks, overlooks the fact that all these pairs have in common is that they form, respectively, the majority and minority of the population. Even in this they do not have too much in common — Blacks constitute only 12 per cent of the total population of the USA and are heavily concentrated in relatively few areas of a vast continent, while Roman

Catholics constitute more than 30 per cent of Northern Ireland's population and are spread, as we have seen, throughout the entire geographical area of a very small province.

It is not, however, the purpose of this chapter to discuss the merits and demerits of all the analyses so far put forward. In large part this has already been done and the conclusions are readily available in an easily-accessible form. The objective here will be to examine three closely related explanations, which could best be described as 'politico-cultural', and one *very* different analysis which concentrates on an examination of social structures from an economic and class perspective and which is based on an academic-ideological viewpoint rooted in the Marxist tradition. These four have been chosen for a number of reasons. The feature that they all have in common is that they are, or purport to be, 'total' explanations of the Northern Ireland problem. They also claim, in their various ways, to have found the path to a solution of that problem. This last point is of crucial importance, sociologically, because the 'explanations' themselves are not simply detached analyses of a complex situation — though they often claim to be just that. They are also powerful instruments in affecting the situation itself. By enunciating the solution as part of the analysis of the problem they are helping to form or maintain ideologies which deeply influence the actions of some members of the society which they are examining and explaining. In this respect, these interpretations of a complex problem in fact become part of that problem themselves and so form an essential ingredient of the analysis that this present work is attempting to make. One final characteristic that these four approaches have in common is that they show what is, at best, a lack of understanding of, and, at worst, a contempt for, the wishes and aspirations of the majority of the population of Northern Ireland — the Protestants. The situation of the latter, in respect to their aspirations and the ideology upon which these are based, will be considered at some length in the next chapter. The point should be made now, however, that those explanations of the Northern Ireland problem which, in spite of the searching criticisms made of them, still are most potent in influencing opinion outside of Northern Ireland and thereby in affecting the social situation within the province, are far from sympathetic to the Protestants. Sociologically, this is of substantial significance in confirming the sense that the majority here have of being beleaguered and in developing sets of attitudes, motivations and actions based upon that sense.

The first of these 'politico-cultural' interpretations sees the problem of Northern Ireland in traditional Irish Nationalist terms.[1] The exponents of this approach have developed their analysis by using the sense of nationalism which grew in parts of Ireland, and among some sections of its community, in the eighteenth and nineteenth centuries as a base for going backwards and forwards in history. A picture is built up of an Irish nation subjugated and divided by many centuries of conquest and unable to fulfil its own destiny because of the dominating presence of a succession of foreign invaders. Chief, and most successful among the latter, were the English who attempted to impose an alien rule and culture upon Ireland. This was resisted over a long period of time, at first without any great degree of success. Finally, however, in the second quarter of the twentieth century, Ireland was able to defeat the English invader — by now 'British' rather than English — and establish itself as a nation in its own right. But the victory was not complete. The nation of 'Ireland' did not correspond with the geographical entity of Ireland because part of one of its provinces — Ulster — still lay outside the jurisdiction of the national government in Dublin. Ireland, therefore, is still not whole, united and free of occupation by an alien power, and will not be until the border is removed and the six occupied counties restored to the motherland. All legal and constitutional means should be taken to achieve that end. If and when it is achieved, not only will national and historical justice be done but the 'problem' of Northern Ireland will be solved and peace will be restored to a troubled land.

In order for this to take place, of course, the State of Northern Ireland will have to be dissolved and the citizens merged into the State of all-Ireland. Objection may be raised at this point to the effect that the majority of those citizens — the Protestants — do not want this process to occur. They have demonstrated time and time again that they are resolutely opposed to becoming part of an Irish union under the rule of a Dublin government and are prepared to take any steps necessary, including physical force, to prevent such an event taking place. How are the wishes of these people to be respected and taken into account and, at the same time, the Nationalist stance preserved intact? Stated baldly, like this, the dilemma the Nationalists find themselves in has no solution. You cannot, at one and the same time, achieve within a society an objective which runs counter to the wishes of the majority of its citizens and also respect the integrity of those citizens. The Nationalist solution to this puzzle is to explain away the Protestant position on two grounds, either or both of which may be used as the occasion demands.

The first tactic is to employ the argument that the Northern Ireland State should never have existed in the first place. It was established only to protect the interests of an alien group who were forcibly 'planted' in the north-east of Ireland almost four hundred years ago and who were given land that rightfully belonged to the indigenous inhabitants. The latter were forced off their holdings and kept in subjugation for a long period. They were denied their rights and made to occupy the least fertile and most impoverished areas of Ulster, while the newcomers prospered under the protection of successive British governments. That protection enabled the Protestants to thrive and to develop traditions which made them different from the other inhabitants of Ireland. Thus, when the time came, in the twentieth century, for them to be incorporated into a united, independent Ireland, they refused and opted instead for a semi-autonomous state of their own closely linked with Britain. As a consequence, the argument goes, the Protestants of Northern Ireland do not have the right to hold up progress towards a united Ireland. The area they live in was illegally occupied by their ancestors and they remain only by the grace and favour of the Irish people. The Ulster Protestants constitute a minority of those Irish people, even though they form a majority in their own state, and they should not, therefore, be allowed to deny the wishes of the majority for a united Ireland.

The second response is to attempt to make a distinction between the Protestant 'people' and their political leaders. The argument here is that most Protestant people in Northern Ireland are reasonable and peaceable and would not object to being part of a united Ireland where they would be well looked after. The arguments in favour of the removal of the border have only to be made clear to them and they will respond positively, if not enthusiastically, to the prospect of unification. The problem here is that the Protestant 'people' cannot be reached because their leaders will not allow it. These leaders, with support and encouragement from undefined political sources in Britain, strive to retain positions of entrenched power and authority from which they exploit their fellow-citizens, co-religionists and Roman Catholics alike. The continued existence of the Northern Ireland State is of crucial importance to them; it would be very much against their interests to see a united Ireland. They therefore use every possible means to mislead Protestant electors about the nature of the society in the South and to persuade them to oppose any attempt made to achieve unification and rule from Dublin. In this they have been successful for a long period of time. They have been able to persuade their supporters not to listen to the Nationalist case and to continue their support for a Northern Ireland autonomous state. If these leaders themselves could be somehow eliminated, then the Protestant people could be convinced that their real interests lay in merging themselves into the Irish Republic.

The second interpretation of the 'Northern Ireland problem' is the one that is adopted by militant Irish Republicanism.[2] They make a case similar to that of the orthodox nationalists in its interpretation of history and its insistence on the need for the remaining six counties of Ireland to be part of an Ireland united into one undivided state. There are two major differences however, between the Nationalists and the Republicans in terms of their definitions of the problem and the means of solving it. As far as the definition of the problem is concerned, the differences lie in the role each assigns to the influence and intentions of the British government. The Nationalists will admit that Britain

herself sees Northern Ireland as a problem she is anxious
to solve in a manner which, it is claimed, will be in the
best interests of the citizens of the North. For the
Nationalists, of course, those 'best interests' are identified
with a united Ireland; Britain's duty, then, is to recognise
her responsibilities and to ensure that she makes every
constitutional effort possible to restore the six counties to
the South. Those efforts include bringing pressure to bear
upon the aforementioned Protestant 'leaders' to accept
the inevitable and persuade their electorate that breaking
the union with Westminster and accepting the authority
of the Dublin government is the only just and equitable
means of solving the problem. The Nationalists have a
wavering trust in Britain's good intentions in this respect
and, even though signs of impatience show through from
time to time, seem prepared to accept a time-lag in achieving
their objectives and to put their trust in legal and constitutional means of attaining the latter.

   This attitude comes through strongly in the statements
made by the Social Democratic and Labour Party (SDLP),
which is the major contemporary political expression of
Irish Nationalism in Northern Ireland. Irish Nationalistic
sentiments are less emphasised in the public statements of
the SDLP than they were in the rhetoric of their predecessors,
and more attention is paid to social reform which will benefit
both Protestants and Roman Catholics. Nevertheless, there is
still an insistence upon the achievement of the unification
of Ireland as an end in itself, coupled with an assumption
that the British government desires this also and will support
measures towards that end. Thus, in the early seventies the
SDLP issued a pamphlet entitled *Towards a New Ireland*
and subtitled *Proposals by the Social Democratic and
Labour Party* (Belfast, undated). This policy statement
outlines in general terms the type of social and economic
measures that the party would like to see implemented, but
in terms of constitutional reform it is very specific and contains the proposal that

   . . . An immediate declaration [be made] by Britain that
   she believed that it would be in the best interests of all

sections of the Communities in both Islands, if Ireland were to become united on terms which would be acceptable to all the people of Ireland and that she will positively encourage the prosecution of this viewpoint.

Such a 'declaration' should be accompanied by 'The creation of Democratic Machinery in Ireland to implement the terms of the above declaration by the agreement of the people of Ireland, North and South.'

The emphasis, thus, is on constitutional reform aimed at a removal of Britain from Northern Ireland, but in a peaceful and orderly fashion and over a period of time. In this fashion it is hoped that an acceptable and enduring solution may be found to a problem of long standing.

The Republicans, on the other hand, adopt a very different approach to the British government's role in the problem. For them, Britain is simply an occupying power which is still subjugating a section of Ireland and ignoring the wishes of its people.[3] Britain has no good intentions towards Ireland, North or South; the country exists simply to be exploited by the imperial Parliament at Westminster to serve its own ends. The 'problem' of Northern Ireland, then, is a straightforward one — it is a country held under colonial rule which denies its inhabitants the right to freedom and the means to achieve their just aspirations. The battle, then, is between Republican patriots and British imperialists. The problem of Northern Ireland will not be overcome until British rule is broken and all traces of the foreign occupation removed. These 'traces' include, in particular, the British Army which is both symbol and means of subjugation of the 'people' by an alien power. The distinction between the Nationalists' and the Republicans' definition of Britain's role in the Northern Ireland problem also dictates the distinction between the means each group adopts in order to solve that problem. As has already been indicated, the Nationalists tend to favour legal and constitutional means and avoid violence. The Republicans reject these as being naïve and inappropriate, and they rely, instead, upon extra-legal means and physical force to achieve their objectives.

This tradition of Republicanism still persists but expresses itself in different ways. Its 'purest' form is to be found in the statements emanating from the *Republican News* and in the rhetoric of Provisional Sinn Féin, the political wing of the Provisional IRA. Attention was focused upon this group in 1981 because of the hunger-strikes at the Maze prison in Northern Ireland — the H Block campaign as it came to be known. A great many public statements were made by the group, at meetings, in the press and in television interviews, and the same theme was constantly emphasised — the overthrow of British imperialism and the achievement of Irish unity. Stress was constantly laid on war and violence in the struggle against the 'Brits'. No coherent policies of economic or social reform have been put forward by this particular brand of extreme Republicanism, though there have been vague references to what will constitute the Irish republic after the imperialists have been defeated.

There are other branches of Republicanism which are less extreme in their willingness to use violence to attain their ends and which do include some form of social and economic programme welded into the demand for Irish unity. Nevertheless, the need for immediate rejection of the British imperialistic presence is constantly emphasised in blunt and uncompromising language. As an example of this, we may take the general stance of the Republican Clubs, as expressed in a statement entitled 'Freedom Manifesto for the Seventies', issued by the McKelvey Republican Club (Belfast, undated). This pamphlet enumerates social reforms and a 'socialist' policy but emphasises as well that

> The need to re-unify the nation dominates the immediate horizon. No demand should be formulated without this in mind.
>
> Any reforms sought by agitation within these structures must be such as (a) to weaken imperial control (whether direct or socio-economic), (b) to strengthen the organisation of the people, (c) to develop all-Ireland linkages at basic level.
>
> Such reforms are in essence revolutionary, because they open up the option of sweeping away, at a later date, the foreign imposed State structures and replacing them with revolutionary-democratic State structures based on the people's organisations.

This line of argument is supported by other groups. Clann na hÉireann, for example, in their publication *Battle of Belfast* (London, undated), produce a political statement which firmly links the battle for the republic with the attainment of rights for the 'workers', and a pamphlet issued by Official Sinn Féin — *Sinn Féin Yesterday and Today* (Dublin, 1971) — expresses precisely the same sentiments.

In general, then, it may be said that Provisional Sinn Féin emphasise unification and the overthrow of imperialism and advocate the use of force to achieve both. The other groups mentioned indicate concern for revolutionary social reform but also emphasise unification and anti-imperialism. Though they do not advocate force, the latter consistently use rhetoric like 'agitation' and the 'sweeping away . . . of foreign-imposed State structures and replacing them with revolutionary-democratic State structures . . .' which, at the very least, imply that force may be necessary at some future time.

Again, as with the Nationalists, the question may be raised as to where do the wishes and aspirations of the majority of the population, the Protestants of Northern Ireland, figure in the Republicans' scheme of things? The simple answer is that they are not taken seriously at all. It would be be hard to realise from a reading of the rhetoric that accompanies the Republican campaign that there *are* any Protestant citizens of Northern Ireland who are strenuously opposed to unification with the remainder of Ireland, let alone comprehend the fact that the latter constitute a substantial majority of the State. When they *are* referred to their existence is explained away in the context of the argument against imperialism. The Republican stance towards the Protestants is similar to that of the Nationalists but even less sympathetic. Britain, so the argument runs, established an alien group of settlers in the north-east of Ireland centuries ago in order to protect her interests. These settlers were to provide a sympathetic population which the imperialistic invader could use as a base to assist in the subjugation of the native Irish. The descendants of these settlers still remain in Ireland in the late twentieth century and are still performing the function that they were originally intended for — i.e. they act as the agents of imperialism. The

Protestant population in the North, then, are catspaws of the British and are being used as the lackeys of Westminster. They are thus not to be treated seriously as fellow-citizens unless and until they recognise their 'real' status and reject it in favour of becoming part of the movement for a free, united and republican Ireland. Again, some attempt is made to distinguish between the Protestant 'people' and their political 'leaders'. It is the latter who are mainly responsible for maintaining the union with Britain in order to protect their own positions of power, and who are, somehow or other, able to persuade the Protestant electors to support them, against the latters' own interests. But in general it would be true to say that Protestants are not recognised as having aspirations and expectations of their own for which a case may be made. They have no integrity as a group.

The third explanation is related to the previous two in that it provides part of the context from which they have both emerged. This is the interpretation of the problem of Northern Ireland as being the inevitable result of the clash of two 'cultures' trying to co-exist within the same society. The definition of the term 'culture' in a sociological sense will be returned to later. At the moment it will be used in the same way as the exponents of the 'cultural' argument use it — i.e. to identify certain aspects of historical tradition which influence art, literature and recreation, at one level, and religious belief and political ideology at another. Culture is, of course, transmitted through education in both its 'informal' and 'formal' senses and the question of the 'formal' method of education — expressed through separate school systems in Northern Ireland — will be taken up at various stages in the book.

The cultural explanation pivots upon the argument that there is a specifically 'Irish' culture which is the true inheritance of the minority group in Northern Ireland and that this culture is not able to find its true expression. It cannot find its true expression because it is clamped into a society which is artificially constructed and contains another and alien culture, called British and characteristic of the majority of its population. There is thus bound to be constant conflict in this society — Northern Ireland — until the heritage of Irish culture, which is the life-style of the majority of the inhabitants of Ireland, is allowed to predominate over the remaining elements of British culture. The latter, then, will quietly wither away.

No attempt will be made here to unravel the complexities of 'British' culture or to highlight those salient features which make it different from any other. This would be a wearisome and probably unrewarding task. The growth and development of a belief which has come about in comparatively recent times in a distinctively Irish culture, has been dealt with admirably by a number of authors including F. S. L. Lyons (Lyons 1973, pp. 224-46). I have used this author's work as the basis for some of the points made in this chapter. Irish culture, so the argument runs, expresses itself in many ways which influence the lives of its people and produce those who are distinctively 'Irish'. There is, first of all, the Irish language which, though not the common language of the present-day inhabitants of Ireland, still is spoken by a minority and must be preserved. Upon its preservation depends not only the welfare of those people who rely upon it for day-to-day communication but also the ability of all to maintain links with Ireland's literary and artistic heritage. For this reason, the minority population in Northern Ireland are constantly encouraged to respect the language and, if possible, to learn it. Irish is part of the curriculum of Roman Catholic schools in Northern Ireland and organisations exist to encourage adults to continue and develop their knowledge of the language. In harmony with this emphasis on the language, the playing of games considered native to Ireland is strongly encouraged and sports like hurling, camogie and Gaelic football thrive among the Roman Catholic population. Thus is emphasised, at one level, the cultural distinction between them and the majority population of Northern Ireland who do not learn Irish and who play 'British' sports like soccer and cricket.

The distinction is vividly expressed in the following quotation from the 1970 edition of the Rule Book of the Gaelic Athletic Association, one of the contemporary organisations which is most powerful and most effective in keeping alive 'cultural nationalism' in Ireland. The close link between 'cultural traditions' and the political expression of Irish nationalism is obvious in the language used:

> The games are more than games — they have a national significance ... The primary purpose of the GAA is the organisation of native pastimes and the promotion of athletic fitness as a means to create a disciplined, self-reliant, national-minded manhood which takes conscious pride in its heritage of unrivalled pastimes and splendid cultural traditions, as essential factors in the restoration of full and distinct nationhood.
>
> The overall result is the expression of a people's preference for native ways as opposed to imported ones ... today, the native games take on a new significance when it is realised that they have been a part, and still are a part, of the nation's desire to live her own life, to govern her own affairs ... until a complete nationhood is achieved, the Association must continue to maintain an all-embracing patriotic spirit ...
>
> This national side of the GAA and its dedication to the ideal of an Irish-Ireland must be kept to the forefront at all times ...

There is no need to elaborate on this quotation; the building-up of a 'national-minded' manhood and the development of a 'preference for native ways as opposed to imported ones' are prime objectives of this 'Athletic Association'. In this sense, the GAA is following in the footsteps of those earlier advocates of the development of Irish culture quoted later in this chapter.

It is, of course, quite possible for two groups to exist in harmony within the same society while displaying cultural traits which differ. The present situation in a number of so-called 'pluralistic' societies in the West demonstrates this. What distinguishes Northern Ireland from these other, more peaceable societies, however, is that the 'Irish culture' propagated by its chief protagonists contains two extremely potent elements — a nationalistic ideology and a set of religious beliefs closely intertwined with that ideology. The nationalistic ideology expresses itself in the the firm belief that the culture of Ireland can only be completely restored and protected when the nation of Ireland extends itself fully to its geographical boundaries. This point was put very forcibly by Douglas Hyde, one of the people most prominent in fostering the idea of a specific national culture when he said:

> In two points only was the continuity of the Irishism of Ireland damaged. First, in the north-east of Ulster, where the Gaelic race was expelled and the land planted with aliens, whom our dear mother Erin, assimilative as she is, has hitherto found it difficult to absorb, and in the owner-ship of the land, eight-ninths of which belongs to people many of whom have always lived or live, abroad, and not half of whom Ireland can be said to have assimilated.[4]

This major feature of 'assimilation' of the non-Irish alien as an essential stage in preserving the Irishness of Ireland is taken up again by D. P. Moran. Moran was a contemporary of Hyde's and one of the most effective polemicists in the campaign for Irish nationalism in the latter half of the nineteenth century and early part of the twentieth. He emphasises the need for the integrity of the 'Gael' to be recognised and says: 'The foundation of Ireland is the Gael, and the Gael must be the element that absorbs. On no other basis can an Irish nation be reared that would not topple over by force of the very ridicule that it would beget.'[5] Irish culture, then, cannot tolerate the existence of any other cultural tradition within its national boundaries. Such a culture must be assimilated or absorbed.

The stances summarised by these quotations lie at the roots of the arguments developed by the 'Irish culture' exponents of the two-culture argument and its application in Northern Ireland. They also powerfully affect the political arguments advanced by the Nationalists and Republicans, which are summarised above. The role of religious belief in the conflict in Northern Ireland will be more fully investig-ated in the later chapters of the book but it is necessary here to touch briefly on some of its more superficial links with the cultural arguments. The part played by the clergy, particularly the higher clergy, in 'Romanising' the beliefs and practices of Irish Catholicism in the nineteenth century has been analysed by a number of historians.[6] At the same time it has been made quite clear that this process of reform of the Irish Catholic Church involved positive encouragement of the development of a sense of Irish nationalism. Crudely put, this was engendered by the belief that the Protestant religion was the religion of the English invader and was therefore the expression of an alien culture. If the integrity of Irish culture were to remain intact, then Protestantism could not be a part of it. Roman Catholicism, thus, was not only to be the one true faith which informed the belief system held by the Irish people, it was also to lie at the roots of Irish culture and to be an integral part of the movement for national independence. Protestantism was to be rejected or, again, 'absorbed'. The point was put, with his customary vigour, by D. P. Moran. Writing in the *Leader*, a newspaper which he founded in 1900, in July 1901, Moran says:

> . . . When we look out on Ireland we see that those who believe, or may be immediately induced to believe, in Ireland a nation are, as a matter of fact, Catholics. When we look back on history we find also, as a matter of fact, that those who stood during the last three hundred years for Ireland as an Irish entity were mainly Catholics, and that those who sought to corrupt them and trample on them were mainly non-Catholics . . .
>
> Such being the facts, the only thinkable solution to the Irish national problem is that one side gets on top and absorbs the other until we have one nation, or that each develops independently. As we are for Ireland, we are in the existing circumstances on the side of Catholic development: and we see plainly that any genuine non-Catholic Irish nationalist must become reconciled to Catholic development or throw in his lot with the other side . . . If a non-Catholic nationalist Irishman does not wish to live in a Catholic atmosphere let him turn Orangeman . . .[7]

Such unequivocal statements of the links between Roman Catholicism and Irish nationalism and the integral parts they both form of Irish 'culture' are not often made nowadays. But the sentiments contained within them are still there and the bonds between religion, ideology and other aspects of

Irish culture are no less strong for being implicit rather than explicit. It is not surprising, then, that the exponents of the 'two-culture' diagnosis of the Northern Ireland problem should maintain that the society which contains both cannot survive without constant conflict, and that they should be tempted by the solution of 'absorption' of the alien, Protestant culture into that of a united Ireland. Unfortunately, both the analysis and the solution suffer from several defects: they neglect the fact that the Protestant majority may be conscious of possessing a religious tradition of their own which they would not be prepared to give up; they neglect the fact that Northern Ireland as a society has existed separately from the rest of Ireland for more than sixty years and may well have developed a culture of its own shared by both majority and minority religious groups; and, finally, they do not recognise the fact that all societies in the West are open to cultural influence from outside their physical boundaries and cannot be imprisoned in one particular period of time.

These three explanations of the Northern Ireland problem have been analysed and criticised in some depth by detached, academic observers and are no longer given much credibility by scholars as acceptable interpretations of a very complex problem.[8] Tending to see this problem as having a single cause, they are too simplistic in nature to explain satisfactorily the social mechanisms which cause the conflict and violence in the society of Northern Ireland. Too many unjustifiable assumptions have been made, for instance, about the aspirations and expectations of the Roman Catholic minority in the North; their support for and involvement in the causes of Nationalism, Republicanism and the preservation of Irish culture is by no means as widespread and unqualified as is believed by the devotees of these causes.[9] The term 'Irish people', which is commonly used in the rhetoric of all three explanations, is a blanket term obscuring more than it reveals. Above all, these three interpretations pay scant heed, let alone respect, to the position of the Protestant majority in the North. They are treated as people to be, at best, tolerated and, at worst, ignored until they are brought to realise that their true destiny lies in being assimilated or absorbed into a united Ireland. They are awarded no recognition as a group with a cultural integrity of their own and, in particular, the importance of their religious beliefs, and the relation these may have to their view of how society should be constructed, is totally ignored.

It should, however, be recognised that, as has been mentioned earlier, these 'explanations' are of significance in that they are actively contributing to the problems of the society of Northern Ireland and helping to shape events here which are significant in prolonging those problems. For example, the survey evidence indicates that the majority of the Roman Catholic population in Northern Ireland do not support the aims and objectives of the extremist and Republican groups but that a minority do. It is evident, also, that within this minority there are people who are sufficiently dedicated to take action to try to achieve those objectives. The form that action takes depends upon which group the activists support; for the Nationalists, constitutional action now consists of moves to involve both the Westminster and Dublin governments in discussions aimed at producing an 'agreed solution', acceptable to all concerned but moving towards a united Ireland. Among the Republicans there are varying degrees of support for a campaign of physical force expressed through the activities of the Provisional IRA.

The tactics employed by both groups have a disturbing effect upon the Protestant majority. As had been stated earlier, there will be no attempt here to catalogue the incidents which have occurred in the last twelve years and which have assisted in the polarisation of the two religious groups. Some examples taken from immediately contemporary events, however, may be used to show how the activities of these groups within the Roman Catholic population and the support they receive from outside Northern Ireland add to the fears and suspicions of the Protestant majority and help to increase their sense of isolation.

If we take the level of 'constitutional' action first, a succession of events early in 1981 will help to illustrate the point. At the beginning of that year, following a meeting between the British Prime Minister, Mrs Thatcher, and the Irish Taoiseach (Prime Minister), Mr Haughey, a series of

joint 'study-groups' was set up to consider matters of interest
and common concern to both countries. This immediately
provoked alarm amongst the Protestant politicians in the
North who suspected that the constitutional position of
Northern Ireland was on the agenda for discussion and that
the integrity of their State was at risk. In spite of repeated
assurances to the contrary, fears grew in some quarters that
Westminster was preparing to 'sell out' Northern Ireland
and arrange a deal with Dublin that would involve the
absorption of Northern Ireland into a united Ireland. These
fears were fuelled by some ambivalent statements from
Dublin about what the talks were about and by the fact that
the Northern politicians were excluded from participating in
them. Reaction amongst Northern Protestant politicians
took various forms, the most spectacular being that led by
the Reverend Ian Paisley. He began a campaign against the
'Dublin Talks', as they were referred to, by holding, under
cloak of darkness, a meeting of some five hundred men on a
hillside in County Antrim at which a pledge was made to
defend the Protestant homeland against any attempt to force
it into the Irish Republic. This was followed by a series of
carefully planned public meetings in a number of towns in
the North at which people were urged to sign a covenant
expressing their loyalty to the Northern Ireland State and
their opposition to any attempt to destroy it. The author
attended the meeting held in Coleraine in March 1981. The
size of the turnout and the strength of the emotion aroused
were powerful demonstrations of Protestant feeling on this
issue. A pamphlet was also issued by the Democratic Unionist
Party (led by Paisley) entitled *Ulster in Peril* (DUP, Belfast,
1981). Its author was Peter Robinson, MP, deputy leader of
the DUP. The pamphlet is subtitled 'An exposure of the
Dublin Summit' and contains such sentences as 'The British
Parliament and Government — once the friends of Ulster, the
defenders of Unionism, and the champions of democracy —
fearing an IRA campaign on the mainland, refuse to do that
which they know is right and just and instead are seen opting
for that which is expedient or pleasing to Irish Republicans'
(p. 3). There is also a reference to 'Republican wolves [who]
are baying for Ulster's blood whipped into a frenzy by the

Prime Minister of the Irish Republic . . .'. This whole campaign — the 'Carson Trail' as it came to be known — was aimed at, and succeeded in, evoking among Northern Protestants memories of the period immediately prior to the First World War when their ancestors, led by Sir Edward Carson, successfully demonstrated their opposition to Home Rule and effectively laid the foundations of the Northern Ireland State.

It is a measure of the profound sense of insecurity among Protestants here that the mere holding of 'talks' in Dublin between Britain and Ireland should provoke such a reaction. This insecurity and feeling of isolation was increased by the total lack of understanding of their feelings in the matter that was shown in Britain. Reaction in Britain to the Paisley campaign varied from complete incomprehension of what the Protestants saw as the issues at stake to contempt at the actions they took. Both attitudes are admirably summed up in a magisterial leading article which appeared in the *Sunday Times* of 8 February 1981. The article is headed 'Ulster Buffoonery' and says:

There are times when inflexibility is a virtue. It is a fair bet that Mrs Thatcher will not be swayed from her modest initiative towards improved Belfast-Dublin relations by Dr Paisley's absurd nocturnal posturings on an Antrim hillside. Nor should she be. The joint studies now on foot between officials in Dublin and London about possible new institutions — new ways of treating common problems — are entirely unmenacing to Northern Protestantism. Indeed, they hold out the only prospect of ultimate peace. It is axiomatic that, just as there can be no settlement in the North without taking account of Northern Catholicism's loyalty to the Irish idea and Dublin, so there can be none that does not command the ready assent of those Northern Protestants who are attached to the union and London.

That still leaves a wide area for useful exploration. Dr Paisley merely stultifies the endeavours of sensible men and encourages fools by his antics. He has been watching too much television about that disreputable buccaneer Sir Edward Carson.

There is no need to labour the point; the effect of such sentiments on Protestants in Northern Ireland can be imagined. The sense of threat under which they constantly live would not be allayed by the stereotyped assurance given in the last sentence of the first paragraph. Rather it would be increased by seeing the activities of the man who has demonstrated at the polls that he has massive support among Northern Ireland Protestants described as 'absurd nocturnal posturings'. And the effect would be multiplied several times over by the contemptuous dismissal of the man who is probably the most prominent 'hero' in Protestant history here as a 'disreputable buccaneer'. All this coming from a journal which is supposed to be the chief mouthpiece of responsible opinion in London, the seat of the Parliament, which has ultimate control over the constitutional future of Northern Ireland.

The sense of beleaguerment is increased, of course, by the activities of the Provisional IRA and the apparent support which they receive from among some sections at least of the Roman Catholic population. Again, only some recent examples will be used. The Provisional IRA are conducting a campaign of assassination against members and ex-members of the Royal Ulster Constabulary and the Ulster Defence Regiment. Both these groups are almost one hundred per cent Protestant in membership, so most of the victims killed are Protestants. The Provisional IRA make the distinction that they are not killing Protestants because they are Protestants but because they are members of the security forces and therefore, by definition, lackeys of British imperialism. The Protestants themselves do not see the force of this distinction; to them it is a more simple matter of members of their own group being killed by Roman Catholics. Events in the early part of 1981 helped again to increase polarisation across the sectarian divide. During the first months of this period a number of members of the Provisional IRA, convicted of acts of violence and imprisoned at the Maze prison outside Belfast, decided to begin a hunger-strike in support of their claim to be treated as political prisoners and not as ordinary criminals. Their action aroused some measure of support among the Roman Catholic population and an equivalent amount of hostility among the Protestants.

The event of major significance, in terms of relationships between the two groups, however, occurred in April 1981. During this month a by-election to the Westminster Parliament following the sudden death of the sitting member, a Republican, was held in Fermanagh and South Tyrone, a rural area where Roman Catholic electors are in a slight majority. One of the hunger-strikers, Mr Bobby Sands, stood as a candidate in the election in a straight fight with a Protestant Unionist candidate. Sands won and the voting figures suggest that the electorate divided almost exactly along religious lines. To the Republicans, of course, this victory was one more demonstration to the British that the 'people' of Northern Ireland rejected their rule and demanded unification with the Irish Republic. There was no mention in their campaign or victory rhetoric of the existence of the Protestant voters in the constituency who so nearly matched the Republicans in numbers. To the Protestants, on the other hand, Sands's victory merely demonstrated that 'Roman Catholics' were prepared to give their whole-hearted support to a member of a terrorist organisation which had been responsible for the deaths of a number of Protestants in Fermanagh and Tyrone. So the divide deepens. A sense of grievance on one side faces a sense of embattlement on the other and conflict continues.

The fourth analysis and explanation of the 'Northern Ireland problem' to be considered here is of a different nature from the other three. The analysis is not expressed by calling upon the ideals of Nationalism or Republicanism or the preservation of Irish culture; this is not to say, though, that it does not have strong ideological overtones within it and has not made its own contribution to the problem it is attempting to interpret. It seeks its roots in the intellectual tradition established by Marx and developed in different ways by various 'schools' of Marxist thought in Britain and on the continent of Europe. Because of the many and various interpretations of what Marx actually meant by what he said and the resulting conflicts between contemporary Marxist scholars it is not possible to speak now of a single 'Marxist' approach to any problem. This is as true of the Northern Ireland problem as it is of any other and Whyte

(1978) has concisely summarised the various Marxist interpretations of the situation and the differences between them.
For the purpose of this work I propose to concentrate
attention on two full-length studies produced by Marxist
scholars – Farrell (1976) and Bew, Gibbon and Patterson
(1979).[10]

Both of these works use the commonly accepted Marxist
focus on any problem of society that is chosen for investig-
ation, i.e. the situation is seen in economic and social class
terms. In terms of Northern Ireland and the conflict which
has characterised its existence as a society, this means that a
seductively all-embracing and relatively simple analysis can
be made. Crudely summarised this amounts to the assertion
that the working class in Northern Ireland, both Protestant
and Roman Catholic, have been exploited by their capitalist
masters who have used religious sentiment to keep the proletariat divided. In a capitalist state, like Northern Ireland,
for the bourgeoisie to retain power to control society and to
exploit the working classes it is essential that the latter be
not allowed to unite. If they do unite, then class solidarity
and 'true' class consciousness will develop among them and
they will become sufficiently powerful to overthrow their
masters and establish a new form of state. Some means, then,
must be found to maintain divisions within the working class
and in Northern Ireland this means was and is religion. The
Protestant working class can be kept not only separate from
but antagonistic to the Roman Catholic working class by a
constant emphasis upon the religious differences between
them. A further refinement is added to this argument by the
use of the 'labour aristocracy' concept. Briefly this means
that one of the ways of keeping the working class from
uniting is to favour one section of it against the other – to
give some workers slightly more privileges than the rest. The
former, then, will cease to have the same concerns as the
latter; it will be in the interests of this 'elite' among the
workforce to support their capitalist masters in order to
retain the slight advantage they have over their fellow
workers. In the case of Northern Ireland, the 'labour aristocracy' idea applies to the Protestants; they are the workers
who have been given marginal advantages over their fellow,

Roman Catholic workers and so it is to the advantage of the former to support their bosses, who are also mainly Protestant, against the latter. In this way the 'divide' in Northern Ireland's society which is causing the conflict is explained. All other factors in the situation — religion itself, political ideology and cultural aspirations — are dependent upon and expressions of this class conflict.

Farrell's analysis is based broadly upon these premises which are elaborated to fit the particular conditions of Northern Ireland. The bourgeoisie are formed out of an amalgamation of British capitalists, who own a substantial share of the manufacturing and commercial enterprises in the North, on the one hand, and, on the other, Ulster industrialists, businessmen and landowners who are united together in the Unionist party. Between them, these two groups brought into existence the State of Northern Ireland in order to protect their own interests. This they do by granting privilege to the Protestant population as opposed to the Roman Catholic minority, in order to guarantee the support of the former and to ensure that they do not make common cause with the latter. The whole edifice, 'Protestant', 'Loyalist', 'Unionist' — Farrell uses the terms indiscriminately, sometimes adding 'Imperialist' also — is held together by the binding force of the Orange Order. The Northern Ireland problem, then, is the result of the creation of a State to serve the interests of a capitalist class who exploit the citizens, both Protestant and Roman Catholic, by favouring the former and suppressing the latter. The solution to the problem is based upon 'a strong, politically-conscious mass movement in the North — and on the mobilis-ation of the Southern masses in opposition both to the collaborationist policy of the government and to the imperialist-dominated economic system' (Farrell, p. 335).

Farrell's book is well-researched and impressively docu-mented. His account, for instance, of the foundation of the Northern Ireland Labour Party and its fluctuating fortunes since its beginning is particularly valuable as an illustration of the near-impossibility of introducing 'normal' politics into Northern Ireland. But the flaws in the analysis are serious. He does not, for example, address the question as to 'why' sectarian fears could be aroused among the Protestant working class and that prevents him from examining whether those fears have any basis in objective fact. Again, Protestants are not allowed any integrity in terms of beliefs or aspirations. One can only assume, from this interpretation, that the Protestant population of Northern Ireland is composed of greedy, self-interested dupes who are content to be manipulated by their leaders in return for small privileges. The Roman Catholic 'masses' are ignorant also, but they have been suppressed and so nothing much should be expected of them yet. This is hardly an acceptable form of analysis of the social structures of a society suffering under the stress of a complex combination of factors which go beyond the purely economic. More serious objection may be taken to the fact that Farrell's work, while having pretensions to scholarship, is heavily influenced by his own personal ideological stance. The author himself says in his Preface that this is not an impartial book and that it is written from an 'anti-imperialist and socialist stand-point' (p. 12). This would have been obvious even without Farrell's admission. It explains why, for example, the Provisional IRA, even though their political ideology is 'confused, incoherent and laced with clericalist anti-communism' (p. 330), are described as 'anti-imperialist guerrillas' (p. 332) while their Protestant counterparts contain 'the storm-troopers and assassins of the UDA, UVF and the other para-military groups' (p. 332).

Such terminology is not really appropriate in a serious work attempting to present an acceptable interpretation of a difficult and confusing set of problems. It does, however, illustrate the author's own ideological commitment and demonstrates the fact that, along with the previous 'explanations', his writings help to contribute to the 'problem' of Northern Ireland itself. Farrell's work, in fact, both reflects and informs the ideology and policies of a small group of political acitvists who combine nationalist sentiment with their own brand of 'left-wing' radicalism. They cannot be identified, yet, as a 'party' but their presence adds another section to the intricate pattern of groups within the North who have offered 'solutions' of one sort or another to the problem of Northern Ireland.

The work of Bew *et al.* also adopts the basic Marxist focus on economic and social factors as being totally responsible for shaping the destinies of mankind and therefore as being the dominant forces operating in the Northern Ireland situation. Their work, however, differs from Farrell's in many respects. Their ideological commitment is to a system of abstract ideas which may have political significance and not to political activism as such and their work is devoted to the elaboration and application of theoretical concepts — with appropriate illustration from empirical data — rather than to a detailed narrative of events. Such work is, of course, an essential prerequisite for any worthwhile sociological analysis because it provides the instruments with which the analysis is conducted. In this respect, the work of Bew *et al.* is impressive.

The basic problem with their analysis is that it starts from the assumption that all 'capitalist' societies are based on class exploitation and that all problems within those societies spring from this. The manner in which those problems express themselves — religious, political, cultural — is simply symptomatic of the fact of class exploitation. The symptoms have no intrinsic significance themselves but must be understood only in the light of the inevitable class conflict which occurs in capitalist society. Therefore we do not look for *causes* of problems in religious, political or other cultural phenomena; these are simply expressions of the real basic cause — the domination by one group in society of a much larger group and the exploitation of the latter by the former. All this in economic terms.

When applying their theoretical framework to the analysis of the conflict between the majority and minority groups in Northern Ireland the authors make this assumption explicit. In their final chapter they state:

It must be insisted that the problem of the 'two communities' is the problem of the reproduction of two class alliances. If this declaration does not immediately illuminate, it still has a consequence which demands careful consideration. The activity of the state in Northern Ireland cannot be reduced to the questions described above. The state had certain peculiarities — as do all states — but it was undeniably a capitalist state. *As such, its basic function was to hinder the unity of the dominated classes.* Conceiving the Northern Ireland state in this way, based on a particular kind of power bloc linked to the maintenance of a particular mass line, dissolves the primacy of the problem of Protestants and Catholics as generic subjects, however often or importantly these ideological forms have been reproduced in the political struggle.[11] (Bew *et al.*, p. 212; my italics)

It should be noted that only if we accept the statement of orthodox Marxism — as conceived by the authors — can we reach the conclusion that the primacy of the problem of whether or not Protestantism and Roman Catholicism as religious belief systems are contributing to the conflict in Northern Ireland can be *dissolved*. We are, in effect, being asked to eradicate a problem by adopting a particular theoretical stance, rather than to confront that problem and attempt to analyse it. In this respect, the authors are doing what so many analysts of Northern Ireland have done — evading the problem of religion by ignoring it or, in this case, 'dissolving' it. The fundamental problem with the analysis of both Farrell and Bew *et al.* is that they are clamped within an ideological structure which both guides and limits the direction those analyses take. They start from the so-called 'orthodox' Marxist stance which will declare that the whole problem in Northern Ireland is the result of a deliberate exploitation of the working class by the bourgeoisie. Taking this theoretical stance, one does not have to define 'working class' or 'bourgeoisie' even in the sense that Marx himself did — Marx who, one suspects, would be affronted by the 'explanations' produced. It is sufficient to confront the problem of a society in change and apply the interpretations which the dogma says have to be the correct ones. In this case, one does not have to ask *why* the separate segments of society challenge one another; one simply has to ask *how* this challenge expresses itself. The problem *how*, in the case of Northern Ireland, is answered by the abundant evidence of violence, death and destruction. The problem *why* is answered by the 'fact' that social classes conflict; this is *inevitable*, because control of the society — Northern Ireland, which is 'undeniably a capitalist society' — is vested only in those who have achieved domination of the economic resources which that society possesses. Thus one avoids the question *why*. It is beyond discussion — it has to be this way. On the basis of this assumption one can avoid or dissolve all sorts of problems, the basic one being that human beings are much more complex than the analysis suggests.

There are some questions which need to be asked at this point. If the whole problem is merely one of a clearly indentifiable class struggle, why is it that although the old Unionist 'establishment' class has been removed from its position of political dominance, the conflict and violence continue? Why, given the fact that we now have political leaders on both sides, expressing the aspirations of both groups, who are both drawn from the same socio-economic class, does the conflict not cease and agreement appear nearer? Paisley comes from the same social class background as the humblest leader of the Nationalist or Republican cause. Is he exploiting them on a class basis? Is the Roman Catholic farmer in County Fermanagh different, in terms of the capitalist structure, from the Protestant farmer in the same county. If not, why do they not join forces and see where their common interests lie instead of confronting each other at the polls and on the streets?

The answer from the 'Marxist' standpoint to these questions is encapsulated in the concept of 'false consciousness'. These people do not realise that they are being exploited by the capitalists and their cohorts. They do not realise this because they have not yet come to the understanding that the millennium cannot be achieved and their full capacity as human beings realised until they have destroyed the people who are exploiting them. Once that destruction has taken place, all will be well. So the problem of Northern Ireland is solved — or would be if the people of that society conformed to the 'ideal type' which the followers of the Marxist school have developed. Both Farrell and Bew *et al.* wish, in their different ways, to educate them — the people — so that they may conform to this ideal type.

The doctrine of original sin is just as helpful in explaining the situation in Northern Ireland.

In the case of Farrell we have an orthodox Marxist interpretation heavily influenced by nationalist ideology. According to this, not only do the 'capitalists', identified as British and Unionist, exploit the 'working class' but they also use the 'Protestant' members of that working class as a means of achieving their ends. It is worth while noting that these working-class Protestants are referred to as 'Loyalists', 'Unionists' or, in the polemic which constitutes the last section of Farrell's work, as 'fascists'. This Protestant working class, who, in classic Marxist terms translated through Farrell, constitute the 'lumpen proletariat', are there to be manipulated, ignored or eliminated according to the needs of the State. They do not accord with the ideal of an Ireland united on socialist principles and therefore are the victims of their own cupidity or stupidity. Adopting this explanation one avoids confronting the possibility that the people composing the society we are examining may have beliefs which motivate their actions and that these beliefs may not be totally dominated by economic expediency. If they were so dominated then the interpretation offered us by Farrell and Bew *et al.* would be accurate; the difficulty then would be that, given the fact that people operate this way, the authors would not have a problem to analyse in Northern Ireland. The people of that society would have recognised their real objective — economic prosperity — and come together in a concerted effort to achieve it. They have not. It is this fact that suggests that something other than their economic well-being occupies their minds.

'False consciousness' can explain this away, without being more helpful than 'original sin' in assisting our understanding. If we say that the human being is alienated from his true self because of the operation of class-manipulated economic factors and that because of this the only way to achieve a true state of peace, happiness and prosperity is to change those circumstances, then we are stating a clear objective for all humanity. To adopt a different but no less comprehensive stance, if we say that human nature is flawed by concupiscence and that because of that we have the problem of achieving in our lives the condition of love for each other which will also produce a true state of peace, happiness and prosperity, we are stating, as well, a clear objective for all humanity. Both are statements of absolutes which may dominate our private lives. This does not necessarily make them accurate guides when we try to understand the lives of other people and their relationships with one another. If we attempt to do this, then we must surely accept that those 'other' people may share dominant values which match our own and supersede the purely material and pragmatic motivations which make up 'everyday life'. In fact, these absolutes may well dominate those motivations and con-stitute the real basis upon which these people live. If they did not, how would one account for most of European history and for the situation in Northern Ireland now? In Northern Ireland, blood is shed because beliefs that people hold demand that it should be. This should be sufficient in itself to throw doubt upon the assertion that the people in Northern Ireland are puppets manipulated by a master called 'British' or 'Capitalist'. It may be more fruitful, in terms of understanding, to regard them as people who are involved in a situation which represents a further stage in the desire to create the circumstances in which they can achieve the aim of living in a condition of peace, happiness and prosperity. This is a positive ideal, not a negative accept-ance of a status quo. In most societies in the West the people have reached a measure of accord as to how this condition may be achieved. They have done this through achieving some degree of consensus about the norms which will enable them all to live together and to attain their objectives. In Northern Ireland this has not happened. One of the reasons why this has not happened may be found in the content of the different religious belief systems which provide the basis of the 'world-view' of the two major and conflicting segments of Northern Ireland's society.

3
The Effect of Religious Belief on the Conflict in Northern Ireland

The preceding chapter examined a number of the analyses and interpretations of the Northern Ireland problem which have been put forward and which have achieved some degree of popular and scholarly acceptance. There have been, at the same time, a number of interpretations of aspects of the problem advanced by scholars, chiefly historians and political scientists, which, while not attempting to 'explain' the whole situation, have nevertheless provided a series of very valuable insights into a confusing set of circumstances.[1] The present work will not attempt to cover the ground already explored but will add what is hoped will be one more insight into the situation. One of the gaps in our knowledge concerns the significant part which religious belief is playing in stimulating conflict and hostility between Protestant and Roman Catholic in Northern Ireland. Most commentators on the scene here do, to be sure, use the terms 'Protestant' and 'Roman Catholic' to distinguish between the two groups, but the words are used basically as labels. A 'Protestant' or 'Roman Catholic' is a person who belongs to the relevant one of these two groups and who holds the political and ideological views acceptable to the group to which he belongs. Thus a 'Protestant' is a person who believes he is 'British', is conscious of a cultural heritage which is British — few Protestants learn the Irish language — and has a great respect and admiration for the British sovereign. He also supports one or other of the Unionist parties, opposes the idea of a united Ireland and goes to a 'church' on Sunday where he worships with his fellow members of one of the non-Roman Catholic sects or denominations. A Roman Catholic, on the other hand, is a person who believes he is 'Irish', is conscious of a cultural heritage which is Irish — if he doesn't actually *learn* the Irish language he does approve of its preservation — and regards the British sovereign as the symbol of an imperial power. He also supports some form of Nationalist or Republican party, is in favour of a united Ireland and goes to a 'chapel' on Sunday where he worships with his fellow Roman Catholics.

The terms 'Protestant' and 'Roman Catholic', then, may often constitute a form of shorthand for distinguishing between two groups, each with a profile of different characteristics. The difficulty here is that in treating these terms simply as labels, however convenient they may be, we run the danger of ignoring the fact that the categories 'Protestant' and 'Roman Catholic' do, in fact, differentiate between two sets of religious beliefs. And that both of these sets of religious beliefs, springing from a Christian foundation, may have profound implications for the manner in which their adherents not only live their daily lives but view society, its nature and the way in which it should be organised. Of particular significance, here, is the question of *how* society should be organised in order to allow the individual the opportunity to hold and practice his religious beliefs. On the basis of this I would maintain that it is important to analyse the content of some of these religious beliefs held by Protestants and Roman Catholics, to demonstrate the social consequences which come from them and to indicate how they are contributing, in some degree, to the present conflict in Northern Ireland.

This is not an easy task. It is often simpler to label people than to explain what those labels mean, and in Northern Ireland it is convenient to divide the two major groups within the society on the basis of religion and style them 'Protestant' and 'Roman Catholic'. It is convenient to do this because whatever differences there may be within the groups in terms of specific brands of politics or social class, their members all have one thing in common — they are either Protestant or Roman Catholic. It thus makes it relatively easy to categorise these different segments of society and this gives the social scientist a flying start in terms of his analysis of that society. But, to state the often overlooked obvious, the terms 'Protestant' and 'Roman Catholic' are *religious* in meaning and content, and therefore have a significance which is based upon the *beliefs* which their adherents hold. Those beliefs, in turn, motivate the lives of the people who are committed to them and this, obviously, means that the beliefs themselves are of fundamental importance in formulating social action. If this were not the case then the labels themselves would be meaningless — we might just as well call the two groups Orange and Green. This being so, it would seem to be of prime importance to look behind the labels at the beliefs and attempt to measure the extent to which they influence the building of social structures and motivate the actions of their adherents. In the case of Northern Ireland this has not yet been done.[2]

One of the reasons why it has not been done is the current disinclination among many sociologists to assign religious belief anything but a subordinate role in the lives of the people they are studying. The classic example of this approach is, of course, to be found in the work of authors who are in the Marxist tradition. Here, it is assumed that not only religion but every form of belief which may be the basis of an ideology is conditioned by the fact of the human being's alienation from his true self through the force of economic circumstances. Religion, thus, is a by-product of the social environment in which its adherents find themselves and does not, therefore, merit particularly serious consideration in terms of the belief system it encompasses. Two examples of this way of thinking and the type of analysis of Northern Ireland's society which results from it have already been quoted in Chapter 2. The point should be made, however, that this analytical focus is applied to all societies and dominates a great deal of contemporary thinking and work on religion by sociologists.

The tendency to give religion a subordinate role in the complex of motivations which inspire human action is not, however, restricted to the writings of social scientists of the Marxist school. It can also be found in the work of scholars who are not in that tradition. Borhek and Curtis, for example, in their valuable work on the sociology of belief (1975), state that 'The cause for polarisation of belief, then, is to be sought either in social conditions, or in someone's attempt to produce social polarisation' (p. 132). The statement is not, in itself, profound. It does, however, demonstrate the point being made here. The authors were not speaking of Northern Ireland but the implication from their observation is that if we are looking for the causes of the conflict which results from 'polarisation' in that society, then we should not seek those causes in the beliefs themselves but in the 'social conditions' which produce them — it being assumed that beliefs are created by social conditions. It follows, then, that the *content* of the beliefs can only be a secondary factor in the process of polarisation because they themselves — the beliefs, that is — are basically the product of social conditions and it is these latter which dominate the lives and motivate the actions of the members of the society in question. Borhek and Curtis follow this line of reasoning which leads them to the conclusion that 'Beliefs persist because groups become *committed* to them, but for commitment to persist, the belief system must be *validated*; validation is largely a social process. . . .' What does this 'validation' mean? It means, in effect, recognition by his peers that an individual's beliefs are acceptable and that, as a result, he will be admitted into full membership of the group which he wishes to join. The compulsion to join such a group is very powerful. There is, on the one hand, the negative fear of social isolation and the barren and solitary existence which that would imply, and, on the other hand, the positive wish to prove oneself as an acceptable human being by being able to make a range of social relationships with other human beings. We all have a need to identify ourselves by being able to say, with confidence, that we are members of some clearly distinguishable group. In order so to identify we need to have our beliefs 'validated'; this motivation is so strong that 'Social identification, then, becomes the dominating criterion of validity of any kind' (p. 133).

If we adopt this analytical stance we can say, in respect to Northern Ireland, that people are Protestants or Roman Catholics because they need to belong to a group which will accept them on the basis of their avowed beliefs. A person's religious beliefs, then, are significant only because they admit him to membership of a group of people which will provide him with the social support systems he needs in order to exist as a member of society. Within this group he finds his identity as a 'social' person; he knows who is like him and, equally important, who is *not* like him. He can therefore identify himself and locate himself in the complex world that contemporary societies now constitute.

This is a very plausible line of argument. The problem with it is that it relegates 'belief' — any belief, including the religious — to a status very much secondary to that of the 'need' for social identification. Belief, thus, becomes simply a symbol of membership of a group and has no integrity in itself — it can be abandoned if the needs of the group change and some other symbol becomes the chief means of achieving and retaining membership and, thereby, identification. This presents a great difficulty because, if this approach to analysis is adopted, it means that we are prevented from examining the actual *content* of the beliefs of those groups. Such an examination can be avoided, or evaded, on the grounds that it is not really necessary because those beliefs are, after all, only a superficial means of gaining entry to a social situation that will fulfil the 'real' needs of the individual. What we are also doing here, of course, is reducing the human being to a mere complex of 'needs' and assuming that the overriding factor which motivates human action is the desire to 'belong' somewhere. That such a desire exists and plays its part in motivating human beings cannot be denied, but it is not safe to assume that this is the only or even the prime factor in motivating action. When it *is* assumed, we get explanations of the existence of the two religious groups in Northern Ireland on the simple basis that they serve the interests of their members by giving them a sense of 'belonging'. The implication is that the religious beliefs have no integrity in themselves but are there to serve this other end by acting as the foundation of a social group.

If this approach is taken, it is not possible to address the question of whether or not the beliefs themselves are playing a vital role in the relationships between Protestants and Roman Catholics. This *does* become possible if one adopts the stance suggested by Weber (1968) when he states:

> It is not our thesis that the specific nature of a religion is a simple 'function' of the social situation of the stratum which appears as its characteristic bearer, or that it represents the stratum's 'ideology' or that it is a 'reflection' of a stratum's material or ideal interest-situation . . .
>
> However incisive the social influences, economically and politically determined, may have been upon a religious ethic in a particular case, it receives its stamp primarily from religious sources and, first of all, from the content of its annunciation and its promise. Frequently the next generation reinterprets those annunciations and promises in a fundamental fashion. Such reinterpretations adjust the revelations to the needs of the religious community. If this occurs, then it is at least usual that religious doctrines are adjusted to *religious needs*. Other spheres of interest could only have a secondary influence; often, however, such influence is very obvious and sometimes it is decisive.
>
> For every religion we shall find that a change in the socially decisive strata has usually been of profound importance. On the other hand, the type of religion, once stamped, has usually exerted a rather far-reaching influence upon the life-conduct of very heterogeneous strata. In various ways people have sought to interpret the connection between religious ethics and interest-situations in such a way that the former appear as mere 'functions' of the latter. Such interpretation occurs in so-called historical materialism . . . as well as in a purely psychological sense.[3]

Weber is therefore challenging the assumption that religious belief is essentially subordinate to other factors in promoting social activity amongst its adherents. He is maintaining that the type of religion that has been 'stamped' upon a society has 'usually exerted a rather far-reaching influence upon the life-conduct of very heterogeneous strata' and that religion is not simply a by-product of the strata within which it is to be found. Religious belief influences, and is, in turn, influenced by the social environment in which it is to be found: there is a complex interplay between religion and other factors rather than a straightforward causal link with religion playing the secondary role.

It is this theoretical stance which will be applied to the role religion is playing in the Northern Ireland problem; we shall not try to 'dissolve' religion as a factor but attempt to estimate, to some extent, the part it is playing, along with other elements, in producing the endless conflict in this society. In the process of this discussion, some attention will be paid to religious beliefs which themselves have direct links with social structures. In this respect, we are following Mehl (1970) when he says:

> One of our basic hypotheses is that Christian communities . . . are societies whose life, practice and type of organisation are determined largely by doctrinal symbols, by convictions of faith, by the *depositum fidei*. This is why we have so often felt it possible to appeal to doctrine in order to account for a sociological reality.[4]

In Northern Ireland, at least, it should be possible to demonstrate that 'doctrine' can, in fact, account for sociological reality.

Protestantism in the province reflects almost the whole tradition of Protestantism in Britain since the Reformation. The Church of Ireland is in the mainstream of the Anglican tradition, the Presbyterian, Methodist and Baptist in the tradition of Dissent, and the remaining small denominations demonstrate the characteristics, dating back at least to the early seventeenth century, of the fundamentalist sects which broke away from the mainstream of Puritanism. All three groups claim membership in the province, regard each other as 'allies' in the face of the Roman Catholic tradition and have common membership in the Orange Order and Unionist politics. There are doctrinal and social differences between them, the Church of Ireland characterised by a sacramental approach to grace and a ritual liturgy that draws support from the upper and lower social groups. The Dissenting bodies, with their emphasis on preaching, the personal encounter with the Divine and simplicity of service, appeal to *all* social groups and particularly to working-class, 'grass-roots' Protestantism which responds to the simple, direct

evangelism, linked with political rhetoric, of the fundamentalist preachers who have been such a significant part of
Northern Ireland's history and whose most celebrated contemporary example is the Rev. Ian Paisley.

The question may be asked as to why these traditions
have persisted in Northern Ireland and still exert considerable influence when, in the rest of the United Kingdom,
they have long since lost most of their force. Posing that
question sheds light on a vital obstacle in the way of understanding Northern Ireland society. Protestants claim that
they are 'British' and that the society in which they have
been dominant so long is 'British' in culture and tradition.
In language and political institutions, this is largely true.
But in other vital areas, Northern Ireland has not had the
same experiences as mainland Britain. Its economy has not
developed at the same rate, it has not experienced the same
working-class political and trade-union movements and it has
not been exposed to the shifts and developments in political
and social ideology which have occurred 'across the water'.
Above all, it has been unique in experiencing fifty years of
one-party rule. This 'one-party' rule has itself been unique
in that it has been sustained by a simple combination of the
religious and the political. The political has been expressed
through the Unionist party which has existed on the single
plank of maintaining Protestant domination and the union
with Britain. In this sense, it has been primarily a defensive
government with little or no political initiative taken on any
of the matters which are the normal concern of the governments of most countries of the western world.[5] The religious
element has been provided by support of the Unionist party
from the combination of Protestant creeds outlined above.
Their contribution has been made more effective through the
organisation of the Orange Order, which has combined the
politico-religious elements. We should look very briefly at
this phenomenon of the Orange Order.[6] Its full title is the
'Loyal Orange Institution of Ireland' and it was founded in
its present form in 1795. The 'Orange' in the title comes, of
course, from William of the House of Orange who is regarded
by Protestants in Northern Ireland as the saviour of their
society because of his defeat of the Roman Catholic James II

in the late seventeenth century. 'Loyal' expresses the loyalty of the members to the British Crown. It is, as one would expect, an exclusively Protestant organisation and is dedicated to the defence of civil and religious liberty. During the last decades of the nineteenth century the Order began to come into its own and emerged as the structure through which grass-roots Protestant opposition to the Home Rule campaign was articulated. It is from this period that its main political significance dates.

The Order has built up a network of local associations — called Lodges — throughout the length and breadth of Northern Ireland. There are, at the time of writing, approximately 1,500 Orange Lodges in the province with a membership variously estimated at between 90,000 and 130,000 Protestant male adults.[7] The structure of the Institution is hierarchical, which accounts to a great extent for the high degree of control which its leaders can exert over the membership. The local Lodges are attached to district Lodges which, in turn, are linked to county or provincial Lodges. At the top of the structure are the Grand Lodge and the Central Council; links between each rung on this ladder are maintained by the officers of each Lodge who send delegates to the next group up the scale. The religious character of the Institution is maintained by the presence in each Lodge of a chaplain whose influence is considerable. In this respect, the Order provides Protestant clergy with a means of enjoying political influence without having to belong to a political party.

In social class terms, the Order is Protestant society in Northern Ireland in microcosm. Its membership links all classes and the top echelon is composed of leading figures of the Protestant political, religious, industrial and commercial elite. As a result, the 'Orange' influence on Stormont, on the Protestant political parties and on the running of the Northern Ireland economy has been very considerable. This has enabled the humbler members of the Order to feel very much part of a power structure which has a great say in the way things are run in Northern Ireland, and in that respect, such members gain much more satisfaction than they would from a political party. By the same token, Orange members of Parliament are able to benefit from a constant source of 'grass-roots' opinion in their constituencies — a much more reliable source than a local party organisation would be able to give them. The Institution, then, draws upon a mixture of combined elites at the top and broad 'popular' support at the base, and it is this which gives it its considerable political and social influence. The Order has been able, through structures which operate — through its Lodges — from street level to district level, to county level and to province level, to provide solid support for the Unionist party in every level of Protestant society in Northern Ireland.

No other part of the United Kingdom has experienced a politico-religious tradition such as this. The nearest parallel — and that an exceptionally crude one — would be the links between religion and government in sixteenth- and seventeenth-century England, where it was possible to identify allegiance to Rome with disloyalty to the State. To push the comparison very far, however, would be absurd. English governments of the time were concerned with problems of welding together a nation state and dealing with constant external pressures which put them in a different order of existence from the Unionist government at Stormont. In Northern Ireland we have a situation where a small province is occupied largely by descendants of people who were established there by a mother country in order to defend her interests, at a time when religion was a crucial *political* consideration, and who still exist in that tradition. But the problem now is not to defend the interests of the mother country — a call that gave them such comfort and security in the past because there was always this comforting giant to turn to for succour and strength — but to defend themselves and their homeland. The Protestants in the North, then, still see the problem in the terms in which their homeland was established: Roman Catholics are still the enemy because Roman Catholics seek to overthrow the State, to deprive them of their homeland. Politics, then, becomes a simple matter of protecting the Protestant homeland, and Protestantism remains the religion which it was in early post-Reformation England — a bulwark against the imperialism of Rome on the one hand, and a defence of the purity of the Christian faith against the errors of Popery on the other. The *Protestant Telegraph* of September 1980, for example, has the arresting headline 'The Pope's Order, Murder Queen Elizabeth'. It is only after reading the article beneath the headline that one realises that the pope referred to is Gregory XIII, the year 1580, and the queen Elizabeth I. The same issue contains an article entitled 'Ten Reasons why the pope should not be invited to make a state visit to Britain'. In summary these 'Ten Reasons' reflect the fear that such a visit would constitute a threat to Protestantism and advance the Papacy's imperialistic designs. A politician in Northern Ireland, then, must be aware that he will only retain the support of his constituents if he is seen to interpret his politics in this religio-political light and to act on that interpretation. How else explain the enormous influence of Paisley as an individual, and the Orange Order as an organisation?

So the Protestant culture in Northern Ireland, with which we are dealing, is unique. Politics in the North is not politics exploiting religion. That is far too simple an explanation: it is one which trips readily off the tongue of commentators who are used to a cultural style in which the politically pragmatic is the normal way of conducting affairs and all other considerations are put to its use. In the case of Northern Ireland the relationship is much more complex. It is more a question of religion inspiring politics than of politics making use of religion. It is a situation more akin to the first half of seventeenth-century England than to the last quarter of twentieth-century Britain.

One perspective, then, on Protestant Northern Ireland would be to see it as a beleaguered group of people determined to defend a tradition and a homeland which they see as under constant threat. Viewed from this angle we observe a society which has all the external trappings of a modern, orbanised, class-structured group, but which basically has one major division around which all other divisions cluster — religion. Much of the bewilderment on the part of observers of Northern Ireland seems to spring from the non-recognition of this. These observers come largely from western 'pluralistic' societies where the actual existence of the state is no longer in question, where some form of open democracy in political institutions is taken for granted, where the members of the society feel reasonably secure in pursuit of their personal and economic goals and where, as a result of all this, these same members have the basic self-confidence to allow the existence of 'deviant' groups within their midst, providing the latter do not seriously challenge the bases on which this self-confidence exists. In such a context it becomes extremely difficult to envisage a situation where religion, with its apparent 'otherworldly' connotations, may become a serious ground for suspicion and mistrust. Religion, in such a pluralistic society, becomes merely a mark of individuality, a private idiosyncrasy, a memory of ethnic tradition or a means of comfort and protection against the demands of life. It is certainly not a reason to be deflected from the serious business of life, still less a cause of conflict of such magnitude that it should result in death, desolation and the destruction of society. Why, given the history of Western Europe since at least the sixteenth century, observers should make this assumption, is not clear, but it is not the purpose of this work to address that particular question. But the non-realisation of the role religious belief can play in terms of human priorities may help to account for the fact that so many commentators are bewildered by observing that class affiliation may *not* be the most important unifying force among people and that economic considerations do not always loom quite so large as may be supposed in the individual's view of his destiny.

It may be appropriate, at this point, to take note of another related problem in viewing the situation in Northern Ireland. It is frequently stated that at no time in the present dispute have Catholics and Protestants attacked each other on doctrinal grounds. This has been taken as conclusive evidence that it is not a religious conflict that is taking place. It is not difficult, with respect, to show the superficiality of this view. The major differences between Protestants and Catholics in their view of Christianity are doctrinal statements which have, in themselves, enormous social and political repercussions. The fact that they are not always made explicit — except by the Rev. Ian Paisley and, more significantly, perhaps, by the Rev. Martin Smyth (a Presbyterian minister and Grand Master of the Grand Lodge of Ireland) — does not make such convictions any the less important. The doctrine of the individual's access to grace may serve as an example here. The Roman Catholic doctrine that grace is to be achieved through prayer and the sacraments, but particularly the latter, has substantial social implications. If the sacraments are essential — Baptism, Penance, the Eucharist (Mass) etc. — the person who administers them becomes of crucial importance. Such a person must be chosen and consecrated — hence the need for a priesthood. The role of the priest is to bring grace, through the sacraments, to the people. Initially, such a priest is an itinerant who combines preaching with his sacramental duties; but as the number of converted grows and becomes geographically widespread, it becomes necessary to introduce an element of organisation into these activities. This is not the stage at which to enter into a discussion and analysis of the development of the Roman Catholic Church through the centuries. The point, however, should be made that because of the doctrine of sacramental grace and the function of the priest as its indispensable mediator we now have the social organisation of parishes and dioceses, governed by an ordained clergy of various ranks, which is the familiar appearance of the Roman Catholic Church. In such a situation the role of the priest has, under the pressure of external conditions, evolved into that of priest-community leader, priest-senior bureaucrat, priest-prince and even that of priest-monarch.

It is not necessary to labour the point of the social implications of these developments. In late twentieth-century Northern Ireland what these in effect mean is that the Roman Catholic clergy have reached a point where, through their sacramental role, they in fact control parishes and a school system, and exercise a control over their lay members which represents a frightening monolith to an outside observer.

The Protestant stance on this doctrinal issue — and hence, the social implications involved — is very different. The Church of Ireland has, to some extent, followed the tradition of Roman Catholicism in terms of its interpretations of grace through the sacraments, but has not pursued its implications in terms of endowing its priesthood with anything like the other's status in terms of religious and social authority. The Dissenting Protestants have a contrasting tradition. For them there is no need of the priest as an intermediary; the duty of the minister of the gospel is to preach in order to prepare the individual for direct contact with the Divinity, and it is through this contact that grace is achieved. There is, therefore, no need for a highly structured clerical organisation dominating its lay members and holding over them the threat of denial of access to grace. Such an organisation, in fact, is seen as a perversion of Christianity precisely because it arrogates to itself the right to stand between the individual and God. The existence of such an organisation threatens Christianity because of its denial of the right of the individual to approach God direct. Because of its power in terms of control it constitutes a very real threat to the existence of Reformed Christianity and, equally important, is able to exert a controlling — if hidden — influence over the *political* institutions of the society in which it operates. Looked at this way, the doctrinal stand of the Roman Catholic Church poses a very real threat to the existence of Protestant Northern Ireland.

It is not, therefore, accurate to say that religious doctrine plays no part at all in the conflict in Northern Ireland. It follows that it is even less satisfactory to conclude that 'religion' in the Northern Ireland context is not 'real religion' at all — otherwise why would Christian be killing Christian — but some form of tribal symbolism, some empty shibboleth by which one identifies friend or enemy. The danger of this approach is that it leads observers to over-emphasise other contributing factors to the conflict; as Darby puts it, in another context, to build their houses of twigs while the logs of Ulster are lying around in plenty.[8]

The Protestants in the North cannot be reduced to a single stereotype. One problem is that they are not taken seriously, in religious terms, at all. The vast bulk of historical writing on Ireland has either completely ignored the Northern — and Southern — Protestants altogether or has regarded them, in Durkheimian or Parsonian terms as an unfortunate 'residual' or 'pathological' element preventing the integration of the society of Ireland in its most meaningful way, i.e. through religion. The Northern Protestants constitute the last barrier to the 'integrated' Ireland of the future. They are an unfortunate hindrance to a solution of a wearisome problem. If they would only realise that they would be welcomed into a united Ireland and treated as equal citizens, then the troubles would be over. Why won't they do this simple thing?[9]

Part of the answer to the last question is that it is *not* a simple thing to do. How complex it in fact is one can gather from applying the analysis of one of the latest and most insightful works on the 'Irish problem' recently produced by a historian. O'Farrell (1971), bases his analysis of the problem between Britain and Ireland on a recognition of the fact of the importance of religion as a causal factor in the age-old dispute. He talks of 'Ireland's English Question' and states that

> The *political* quarrels of the Irish were largely among themselves. Ireland's dispute with Britain, however much it was within the realm of politics, was not about politics. The quarrel with Britain was not about what they had in common, but what was held in difference — a total world view. This world view was composed of several closely integrated elements — race, culture, temperament perhaps, historical experience and development, and religion; with religion both pivot and linch-pin. These are the essential foundations, upon which the political activity and ideologies of the 19th and 20th centuries are so much mask and overlay (p. 3).

Later O'Farrell says:

> Too little attention has been given to the possibility that political solutions were insufficient because the problem was not essentially political. It was historical and religious, and a problem of identity. To the Irish, British government both represented and continued to perpetrate a crime against their selves, their history and their religion (p. 7).

This analysis represents a very valuable insight into the

operation of Irish society and its relationship with the larger British society of which it was, unwillingly, a part. Furthermore, Professor O'Farrell does not fall into the error of neglecting the importance of ideologies — nationalism being the most obvious one — which have played a part in the dispute, even though these 'ideologies' may themselves be rooted in religion — this 'total world view'. Nor does he neglect the economic variable, which one school of scholarly analysis would emphasise over all others.

The major disappointment in O'Farrell's work is that he does not apply his analysis of the importance of religion to the Protestants in the six counties of the north of Ireland. He speaks only of Roman Catholics in Ireland, in this vein. If, quite rightly, he emphasises the importance of religion in what is now the Republic of Ireland, then logic would demand that he do the same in the province of Ulster. Instead, in his section on the North, O'Farrell (1971, pp. 300-11), while paying some attention to the significance of religion as a dividing factor, speaks of Northern Ireland as a 'historical fossil' (p. 300) and of 'popular religion — particularly that form of it held, or residually held, by the socially ascendant group — [as not evolving] past the age of the wars of religion, the seventeenth century. The fossil has lived so long that its living complexion seems but a mask' (p. 304). Finally, O'Farrell's comment on Prime Minister O'Neill's election manifesto of 1969 is worth quoting. 'To assume', says O'Farrell, 'that economic interests and peace rated higher priorities with the Ulster minority than principles and emotion, than Catholicism, and nationalism and history and justice and hatred, was fatuity rather than creative hope' (p. 301).

This comment may well be correct. It does not assist us, however, in any attempt to understand the present stance of Protestants in Northern Ireland. Let us apply to them the same criteria that O'Farrell has applied to the Southern Irish Catholic majority. It may help to bring a better understanding of Northern Ireland's divided society if we say that the Northern Protestant's quarrel with Roman Catholic Ireland is also based on a 'total world view', a world view itself composed of the integrated elements of race, culture, historical experience and development and religion — again with religion being both 'pivot and linch-pin'.

Contemporary Protestant spokesmen in Northern Ireland make this point clear. In the *Protestant Telegraph*, for example, the mouthpiece of the Rev. Ian Paisley's Free Presbyterians, we have the following statements made:

> Liberty is the very essence of Bible Protestantism. Tyranny is the very essence of Popery. Where Protestantism flourishes Liberty flames. Where Popery reigns Tyranny rules. As Liberty and Tyranny have no common meeting place, so Protestantism and Popery cannot be reconciled . . . Popery is tyrannical in every sphere of life.
>
> . . . On the other hand, Protestantism is the torch bearer of liberty. Protestantism spells liberty in the religious sphere. Protestantism, at a stroke, cuts down all the shackles of superstition and priestcraft. The soul is free to commune with its Maker. There is one mediator between God and man — the man Jesus Christ. Protestantism hands out an unemployment card to every Papist priest . . . The Protestant's home is his castle. He brooks no interference from Pope, priest, pastor, preacher or prelate . . . No one can control the Protestant's education or the books which he shall read. He is free born and trembles not at priestly threats or the Papal curse . . . At the ballot box the Protestant exercises complete liberty . . .
>
> In our province the battle lines between Papal Tyranny and Protestant Liberty are joined . . .[10]

What emerges from this quotation, to illuminate the Ulster Protestant's 'world view', is the emphasis on the importance of the individual's direct access to the Almighty — in contrast to the Roman Catholic doctrine of grace through the sacraments — and the violent opposition to and fear of Roman Catholicism. To the Northern Protestant, a united, Roman Catholic Ireland would be a society in which he could no longer operate as a free individual. It is hardly surprising, then, that he should react violently to the thought of finding himself a member of an underprivileged minority in such a society.

The sentiments expressed in the above quotation from the

Protestant Telegraph are echoed over and over again in Paisley's own writings. The latter are voluminous, and this is not the place for a detailed analysis of their content; a selection from a representative sample should, however, be sufficient to demonstrate the enduring themes — a fierce pride in Protestantism and the Protestant interpretation of Christianity, and distrust of the Roman Catholic Church. They both come through strongly in *Messages from the Prison Cell* (Belfast, 1969), especially in the 'Fifth Letter from the Prison Cell' in *Why I am a Protestant* (Belfast, undated) and in *The Battle of the Reformation, Why it Must Be Fought Today* (Toronto, 1967). Paisley's views on the ecumenical movement are also worth quoting. In his pamphlet on *The World Council of Churches* (Belfast, undated) the latter organisation is attacked on the grounds that it is 'Doctrinally Unbiblical, Basically Unprotestant, Ecclesiastically Unclean, Practically Unchristian, and Spiritually Untrustworthy'. It should be noted, in this connection, that while many Protestant church leaders would not use Paisley's fiery rhetoric to describe their attitudes towards the ecumenical movement, this movement does not flourish in Northern Ireland. There is still deep anxiety among Protestants about any movement towards the 'Church of Rome', believing, as they do, that this Church interprets the ecumenical movement as leading to the eventual submission of the Protestant Churches to the authority of Roman Catholicism.

Objection may be raised, at this stage, to quoting the statements of Dr Paisley. He is, after all, regarded as an 'extremist' and not representative of Protestant opinion in the north of Ireland. Further his Free Presbyterian Church only accounts for a very small, if growing, minority of Protestants in the province. The strength of this objection is recognised even though the extent of grass-roots support — which is far beyond the membership of his Church — that Paisley commands has been evident on many occasions, not least through the success of the Ulster Workers' Council's strike of 1974, in which he played a major role. There are also the facts of his continuing resounding successes at the polls and his status as an elected representative of Northern

Ireland at the European Parliament. By any objective standards it would be hard to demonstrate that Paisley is a
'maverick' or a demagogue, and that, as such, he is unrepresentative of Protestant opinion in the province.

Nevertheless, extra evidence needs to be adduced to help
to clarify the position of Protestants in the North vis-à-vis
the opposing world view of Roman Catholic Ireland. There
are many sources from which this evidence may be gathered.
One of the clearest, most balanced and effective statements,
however, comes from the previously mentioned Rev. W.
Martin Smyth. In an article entitled 'A Protestant looks at
the Republic' in *Sectarianism — Roads to Reconciliation*,
Smyth carefully elaborates the Protestant position in this
respect. He begins by talking of 'Protestants' in general but
quickly brings his focus to bear on the particular problem
in Ireland. He says:

> . . . in practice the term 'Protestant' is generally used
> simply to refer to any professing supposed Christian
> who is not a member of the Roman Communion . . . this
> means that, among the people described as Protestants,
> there is vast variety. Not only is there great variety in
> temperament, teachings, attitudes and atmosphere as
> between Presbyterians, Anglicans, Methodists, Congreg-
> ationalists, Unitarians and so on, but there is also great
> variety within each of those churches or groupings. There
> are those differences between fundamentalists and
> modernists, high church and low church and many more.
> And there is scope for all sorts of 'individual eccentricities'
> (p. 27).[11]

The Protestant in Ulster therefore finds that, even though
he may let himself be guided in religious matters by the
particular traditions prevailing in the Church to which he
belongs, he cannot fail to be aware that in those matters
there are 'many authorities, many points of view'.

Smyth proceeds to develop this last point to show that
great pressure is thus put on the Protestant to decide where
he stands without depending much on some one authority.
In any matter of religious authority he does have, to some
extent, to make his own decisions. And this, in turn, means

that he has to be a consciously consenting participant in what he does.

This is pertinent to our previous point about the 'monolith' of the Roman Catholic Church and the distaste Protestants have for it. Unity among Protestants is *not* monolithic but is more an agreed consensus among believers. Protestant unity is based upon mutual recognition and acceptance among people who differ widely from one another. Because they accept their differences and recognise one another's good faith they can develop a spirit of unity which, says Smyth, is not shared by the Roman Catholic Church. The latter will not come to meet them except on its own terms which the Protestants must accept if they are to be recognised as Christians. Roman Catholics, therefore, appear to many Ulster Protestants as members of an 'idisoyncratic sect of exclusive brethren' (Smyth 1974, p. 28).

This expression of the gulf between Protestants and Roman Catholics in Northern Ireland is important enough in itself. Smyth, however, goes further. He points to the variety of human relationships within the various denominational groups as a characteristic of Ulster Protestant life, again in contrast to the monolith of the Roman Catholic minority. He highlights particularly the status of the Protestant clergyman in contrast to that of the Roman Catholic priest. He claims that, in status, a Protestant clergyman is *not* the opposite number of a Roman Catholic priest. The criteria he applies to establish this distinction are basically social. The major differences lie, first of all, in the fact that the Protestant clergyman has to share authority with his congregation and that, as a result, there is a very high degree of lay participation in the work of his Church. Secondly, Protestant clergy are usually married and their wives often play a part of some importance in the social and community life which surrounds and is an essential element of the mission of the Church. In sum '. . . the Protestant clergyman owes his status in the community much more to what he is himself, and the sort of human relationship he is able to establish, than to the fact that he is a clergyman' (Smyth 1974, p. 30).

This, Smyth points out, is in stark contrast to the Roman Catholic Church in Ireland. Where Roman Catholicism prevails there is a situation where the religious and social aspects of whole communities are dominated by a single Church. There is a stress on defining doctrine in words and on achieving uniformity of doctrine, even though the latter is subject to development. Clergy, also, are celibate and do not share their work very much with members of the laity. Further, they form a highly organised structure which imposes a uniform authority in all matters of faith and morals. Finally, to return to a point already made above, these priests, through administering sacraments regarded as necessary to salvation, have a considerable coercive power over those who are believing members of the Church.

Smyth is not alone in his views. He is speaking as a Presbyterian but his attitudes are reflected in the writings of clergy from other major Christian groupings in Northern Ireland. The Reverend Dr M. W. Dewar, for instance, a Church of Ireland clergyman, produced a booklet entitled *Why Orangeism?* (Belfast, 2nd edition 1965) which contains a Foreword by the Right Reverend W. S. Kerr, the Bishop of Down and Dromore. In this publication Dr Dewar says:

> ... there can be no doubt that there is a deeply rooted distrust of the encroachment and ascendancy of the Church of Rome in the heart of Ulster Protestants, which recent events in the Republic of Ireland have done nothing to lessen, in spite of its condemnation of 'illegal organisations'. But the Northern Irishman is impressed by deeds rather than words, and his determination to surrender 'not an inch' of the Border is based upon his unshaken conviction that 'Home Rule is Rome Rule' (p. 17).

In this extract, the *political* influence of the Roman Catholic Church in the Republic of Ireland is being attacked and the determenation of Northern Protestants that that influence should not extend into Northern Ireland is being reinforced. In a leaflet issued by the Loyal Orange Institution of Ireland in 1970 — which is an extract from *The Junior Orangeman's Catechism* (Belfast, 1966) of which the Rev. Dr Dewar was also the author — doctrinal elements of Roman Catholicism are attacked. The leaflet is entitled 'The Qualifications of an Orangeman' and was distributed to all Orange

Lodges. It indicates, among other things, that the Orangeman must

> ... love, uphold and defend the Protestant religion, and sincerely desire and endeavour to propagate its doctrines and precepts; he should strenuously oppose the fatal errors and doctrines of the Church of Rome, and scrupulously avoid countenancing (by his presence or otherwise) any act or ceremony of Popish worship; he should, by all lawful means, resist the ascendancy of that Church, its encroachments, and the extension of its power ...'

Enough evidence should have been quoted, at this stage, to show that Paisley's attitude towards the Roman Catholic Church is not untypical of Protestant views in Northern Ireland. In terms of how far these views percolate through to 'grass-roots' Protestantism, Paisley's popularity should be remembered along with the fact that Smyth is a prominent member of the single largest Protestant Church in Northern Ireland and his views have not been challenged by his fellow-churchmen. By the same token, Dr Dewar's pamphlet *Why Orangeism* sold over forty thousand copies and his *Catechism* had the full backing and approval of the Orange Order, whose significance as a political, social and religious organisation in Northern Ireland we have already demonstrated.

It is not the purpose of this work to comment on the theological validity of any particular religious viewpoint. We have neither the competence nor the desire to do that. Our purpose is to try to produce a *sociological* analysis of a divided society. Our concern is with human action and motivation. Whether or not the Protestant view as articulated by Smyth *et al.* is 'accurate' in the theological sense is not of final importance. What *is* important is that the social group 'Protestant' *believe* it to be accurate and therefore construct their world view and the bases of their ideologies on this foundation. In this connection, what is important is the relationship between the theological stance of Protestantism and Roman Catholicism and the social structures and human motivations thereby created. On the grounds indicated by the authors quoted, there are not two monolithic religious groups facing each other in Northern Ireland. There is one socially monolithic group — the Roman Catholic — and a consortium of other religious goups — Protestants — united on a basis of mutual respect, sympathy and understanding on the positive side, and dislike of the Roman Catholic Church on the negative side. Roman Catholics are themselves united, and therefore part of a social structure, on the basis of *their* world view which shows them an image of themselves as heirs to a tradition and a set of beliefs that give them a destiny and a right as yet unfulfilled. In order to achieve these they are welded into an authoritarian structure which both inspires and confines them in their purpose and, at the same time, makes it well-nigh impossible for them to communicate across the religious divide.

Any sociological analysis of Northern Ireland should, then, take account of the religious factor. Not as simply a 'pathological' feature of a society that knows no better than to adopt empty shibboleths around which to sloganise. Not, either, as simply a useful means of group identification — this is a conveniently facile form of psychological reductionism which does not merit a lengthy discussion (see above). Such an analysis may not, in the last resort, fall back upon the assertion that the problem of the divided society in Northern Ireland is totally an expression of the economic exploitation of the 'working class' by the 'capitalist class', who are using 'religion' (undefined and unexamined) to keep divided and subservient the mass of the population who may challenge their power. Such an explanation falls foul of the temptation to produce an answer which avoids confronting the problem of the non-material motive for action. If one does this it is easy to slide around around the blockage in understanding human motivation by calling into action such explanations as 'loneliness', 'desire for security', 'need for roots', a 'sense of belonging'. These are the reasons, we are told, why members of Northern Ireland society adopt 'religious' attachments.

As we have said already, this type of understanding of the human person underlies many of our analyses of social action. Often, it produces a parody of itself, as when we attribute the adoption of the religious life as due to these causes and then adduce them also as the reasons for leaving it. There is a reluctance among social scientists to accept the concept of *commitment*, or the ensuing fact that people are capable of ordering their actions on the basis of commitment. It is strange that this should be so when there is so much evidence to support a counter-position. Perhaps the legacy that we have of the 'scientific' view of man as a person, which implies that he can only be understood by being viewed as acting on a narrow base of personal, material self-interest (which is what 'rational action' has now come to mean), has intimidated us as social scientists into ignoring that which does not fit into this scheme, or, if not ignoring, then explaining any 'non-rational' action by relating it to some category of 'need', which the rational action has produced.

The 'Protestant' position and the 'Roman Catholic' position in Northern Ireland are part of a long tradition that is rooted in the development of Christian beliefs, and the manner in which they have become articulated with social institutions and the process in which they constitute a culture — a way of life, or a 'world view' — which is of vital significance in motivating the actions of the adherents of those beliefs. This tradition has expressed itself in many ways and in many societies. In most of those western societies, wherein the bulk of sociological enquiry has been concentrated, this religious tradition has been seen as representing itself only in the sense now that it constitutes an increasingly specialised and compartmentalised part of the complex system of motives that dominate human action. It takes its position, and a very insignificant position at that, in the hierarchy of values that dominate human action. Religion, now, is effectively subordinate to the major themes that dominate our lives as members of society; these themes are the achievement of economic and material goals which find their expression in political goals and result in the way in which we finally decide who is to govern our societies. In that situation, religion is important only in our private and secret lives.[12] It may significantly affect the manner in which, if we are parents, we try to bring up our children, or, as individuals with or without children, we find a means to 'escape' into a private world which provides us with the support and succour we need to survive. How we manage to separate our private lives from their public expression is another question, which has been answered to nobody's satisfaction. This standpoint has inspired a great deal of scholarly research and writing on the contemporary position of western societies, their pluralistic nature and the process of 'secularisation' which has taken place within them.[13] It is not our purpose, at the present time, to examine this line of argument or to bring into consideration the work of scholars who have presented a contrary view. All that needs to be said now is that if this analytical stance is adopted, then there is no chance of understanding the 'problem' of Northern Ireland. The forces that are provoking that 'problem' find part of their roots in the religious tradition that has influenced Europe and America at least since the sixteenth century. The peculiarity about Northern Ireland is that the conflict which took place in the remainder of Europe and in the United States some centuries ago is taking place in this province *now*. The other societies have found some means of dealing with that problem and producing a 'modus vivendi' for the conflicting groups. Northern Ireland has not. Some insight into the reasons *why* it has not may emerge from the basic argument of this work. For this understanding we need to look, briefly, into the development of the Protestant and Roman Catholic Christian traditions which have helped to produce the present situation in Northern Ireland and the implications this has for creating the stances not only of Smyth and Paisley and the people they represent but also of the opponents they confront.

The history of the development of Christianity, both before and after the Reformation of the sixteenth century, indicates that the system of beliefs which constituted the theological basis of Christianity provided the social basis for the establishment of a Church.[14] This had profound implications for the culture of the society in which that Church was established because the 'Church' was and is a coming together of the people who believe in the fundamental precepts of the dogma which they are taught, and who base their view of the way in which they should conduct themselves in relationships to their fellows, on this belief. In this way, they are committed, through the faith which they profess, to a set of directives which govern their actions — to a 'worldview' which plays a major part in deciding how they should organise the priorities in their lives and how they should cope with material exigencies and how to bring into being the political structures necessary to govern the societies of which they are a part. In this way they were, originally, differentiated from their fellow members of society and so looked for a form of social organisation — which institutionalised their beliefs — that was clearly distinct from the remainder of the society of which they were a part.

Christianity, then, became institutionalised in a form which distinguished its members — the 'Church' — from the rest of a society. But this institutionalisation was based on a set of beliefs, distinct from those held by their non-Christian peers in the society. In this sense it gave them a total world view which illuminated their ideas about how society should be organised and, at the same time, confronted them with a group of people who needed to be converted to that world view. They had thus a purpose and a mission. Both were expressed through their beliefs. The purpose was to cherish the beliefs which constituted their world view and to ensure that they survived and prospered. The mission was to convert the rest of the members of the society of which they were a part to accepting the validity of those beliefs and, on the basis of them, to construct the institutions — family, political, educational and economic — which would allow their beliefs to come to full fruition. When this was achieved, the City of God would appear in all its earthly fulfilment.

How did these objectives express themselves in social action and the formation of social institutions which came about as a result of the interplay of the beliefs and the social environment in which they operated? Weber, when groping towards this degree of understanding, demonstrated in *The Protestant Ethic and the Spirit of Capitalism* how the elite produced by 'Protestantism' helped the institutionalisation of what we now call the 'capitalist system' to come into existence.

This is but one instance of the manner in which religious belief can confront the other realities of human existence and help to shape the patterns of life within a society of human beings. There are other ways in which this can happen which need to be brought into consideration, ways which are of particular significance to the 'problem' of Northern Ireland.

The chief of these ways is the manner in which a particular Christian belief system relates to the whole notion of the society of which it is a part. In the case of the Roman Catholic Church, the relationship is clear. The *purpose* of the existence of the community of believers that constitutes this Church is to preserve and maintain the *depositum fidei* in its full and entire integrity. In order to do this, orthodoxy must be maintained and enforced; if this is to happen, then a full structure of authority must be erected which can enforce that orthodoxy and operate the sanctions necessary, through the control of the sacramental access to grace, which will influence the members of the Church through granting or denying them the means to salvation. The *mission* of the Church, so conceived, will be not only to spread the gospel of its founder into every level of society, but also to control the manner in which that message is not only disseminated but interpreted. This means that, ideally, the Church must attempt to permeate all the other institutions in society; and not just permeate but, if possible, control them so that the society itself becomes a place wherein not only is the *depositum fidei* preserved but its social potential realised and the City of God achieved. This means *control*, and control not just of the committed members of the Church but also of the means by which the whole society regulates itself — that is, the political institution (government), the family institution (which provides the socialisation for the future members of society), the educational institution (expressed, now, in the formal school system) and the economic institution. The obvious way in which to establish such control is to achieve, literally, the status of an 'established Church', closely identified with the political control of the society in which it is located. The Roman Catholic Church was, *de facto*, in that position and its clergy exercised a great degree of influence not only over their 'flocks' but also over the latter's political leaders. One of the effects of the Reformation in the sixteenth century was to alter that situation and allow scope for another definition of Christianity to put its stamp upon the societies in which its members lived. In most Western European societies the result has been that over the centuries the influence of the Roman Catholic Church over the political and other institutions of society has been weakened. In Ireland this is not the case. The Roman Catholic Church not only re-established itself as a potent force in the development of the culture of the provinces of Munster, Leinster and Connaught in the nineteenth century and helped to form a 'nationalist' ideology in which the 'Protestant' was not acceptable.[15] It also permeated the society of those provinces to the extent that it was officially recognised in the Irish Constitution inaugurated in December 1937 as having a 'special position'.[16] It was, in fact, the established Church, recognised now *de facto* and *de jure*. The community of believers had, through their clergy, attained not only their purpose but also their mission — they had attained the protection of the *depositum fidei* and the control of the social institutions which expressed and manipulated the patterns of the lives of those individuals who made up the society of which they were a part. But the society is not complete and whole; in order to be so it has to encompass the entire area defined by the geographical boundaries of Ireland. Within those boundaries exist the remainder of the province of Ulster which has not been incorporated into the Republic of Ireland. It is inhabited by not only a substantial proportion of people who share, or are assumed to share, the Church's world view, but also by at least twice that number who reject that view and adopt another. These people are 'Protestants'. What is there to do about them? Their 'world view', stamped by their religious beliefs and influenced by their cultural tradition, is 'fossilised'. What does one do with a fossil? Bury it, put it into a museum or use it as an interesting example of life past which cannot possibly influence life present? Whatever one does, the fossil is dead and needs no consideration. The fossil, in fact, lives, moves and has its being.

One further point needs to be made in connection with the view of the Roman Catholic Church of its relationship with the society in which it is embedded.

Although the mission of the Church is to convert the members of that society and to spread its influence into the other major social institutions, it must never forget its purpose — the protection of the *depositum fidei*. This means that the organisation of the Church and the control of its activities must remain separate from that of the State. In effect this implies that although the Church may claim the right to intervene, for example, in the operation of the political institution, it cannot accept the reverse process — the intervention of the leaders of the political institution in the affairs of the Church. In this respect, the Roman Catholic Church cannot become 'established' in the sense that some forms of Protestantism did, because it could not envisage a situation in which a secular political leader was able to have a direct, indeed a controlling, influence over the internal organisation of the Church itself.

This situation is seen in its extreme form in Ireland and helps to build upon Protestant fears of an autocratic clergy. Protestants in the north of Ireland, coming from an entirely different religious background, see themselves confronted in the Republic by a Roman Catholic Church which regards itself as separate from the State and autonomous while, at the same time, claiming the right to intervene in the actions of that State.[17] In social terms, the significant break between Protestantism and Roman Catholicism was over the sacramental means of achieving grace. This particular aspect has already been discussed earlier in this section. The point needs to be made, however, that in social terms, the Protestant view prevailing in Northern Ireland makes the 'true Church' invisible and salvation dependent upon faith alone. This tradition has basically differentiated the religious system from the political system. Though they may interact with each other they do so through the 'persons' of the individuals who are active in both systems and not through the imposition of the will of one organisation upon another. So, Protestant clergymen in Northern Ireland may wish to influence political decisions and to become members of the

State legislature. They do so by submitting themselves to a political process and becoming elected by a constituency, in the same way as any other politician. They do not claim the right *as clergy* and members of an autonomous collectivity to intervene directly in political matters.

Thus, in Northern Ireland there are two groups who, apart from other characteristics, are distinguished by an interpretation of Christian beliefs which has direct social consequences. On the one hand, there is the Protestant view of religion which sees Christians as coming together to form the 'city of the holy'. This city is created by the voluntary cohesion of believers who join together to form a society based upon the creed of a common belief. This common belief is adhered to voluntarily and does not have imposed upon it the dogmatic authority of a hierarchically organised Church basing its claim upon the transmission of grace through its clergy. On the other hand, there is the Roman Catholic view of society based upon a world view which accords *authority* to higher powers, vested in a privileged elite — the clergy. This group can dispense grace through the sacraments and can therefore operate the types of sanctions on the lives of individuals, which no other institution can do. This influence is superior to that of all other institutions — political and economic — and can claim a special relationship of autonomy to those institutions, particularly the political.

In this case, the Northern Ireland Protestants are facing a whole world view which owes a great deal to religious beliefs different from theirs. Their dilemma is real, particularly when it is apparent that the world view in question, and the religious beliefs with which it is articulated, may not only permit but even encourage the existence of a church super-structure of authority that invades the other institutions of society to the extent that it can, for example, forbid a political act in the Republic approved by the elected government and aimed at improving social welfare. It has also proved its effectiveness by imposing its will in various other ways — in connection, for example, with marriage, divorce, contraception and adoption — which offend the Protestant world view and, at the same time, reduce Protestants to the status of second-class citizens. The religious divide in Northern Ireland is not based purely on the symbolic membership of a group with different political ideologies but is rooted in different interpretations of the Christian faith, which, in turn, help to form attitudes as to what 'society' and its institutions should be about.

To demonstrate, sociologically, the contemporary views of Northern Ireland Protestants towards the Irish Roman Catholic Church, it is obviously not sufficient to rely solely upon theory and history. These views are, however, articulated through the journals widely read by committed Protestants and these journals constitute valuable source materials. The *Protestant Telegraph* has already been quoted, but probably the most influential publication is the *Orange Standard* which is the semi-official mouthpiece of the Orange Order. This newspaper appears once a month, and I have done a content analysis of all the issues from September 1979 to May 1981, inclusive. It is not proposed to reproduce that analysis here; what emerges from it, however, is the constant reiteration of the Protestant fear of Roman Catholicism and their consequent determination to defend their belief system at all costs. There are frequent references to the 'imperialistic' designs of the pope and to the sinister workings of the Roman Catholic hierarchy in the Republic. These are often backed by theological articles which focus upon the 'errors' of Rome and the need to be constantly watchful in the defence of true Protestant Christianity. Always there is the reference to the need to protect Northern Ireland as a *State*; its existence as such is essential to the welfare of Protestantism. Some examples may be quoted: in the issue of March 1981, under the headline 'Remember 1912 and 1971' the readership is reminded that in 1971, in order 'to mark fifty years of the State of Northern Ireland 1921-1971 a Covenant was published by the Grand Lodge. It was . . . titled "In Defence of Northern Ireland". 334,000 men and women were signatories to this second Ulster Covenant and that information was relayed by the Grand Master, the Rev. W. Martin Smyth, to the Prime Minister at 10 Downing Street'.

The Covenant begins:

> Conscious of the forces at work for the overthrow of the Province and Parliament of Northern Ireland and convinced that any further interference in or undermining of the internal jurisdiction of the democratically elected government of Northern Ireland would be subversive of our civil and religious freedom and disastrous to our material well being, we . . . do hereby pledge ourselves in solemn covenant throughout this our time of threatened calamity to stand by one another in defending our cherished position of citizenship in the United Kingdom. . . . In the event of the Constitution of Northern Ireland being suspended or abnegated against the will of the people, freely and democratically expressed for half a century, we further solemnly pledge ourselves to work unremittingly for its complete restoration without tie or bond.
>
> In sure confidence that God will defend the right, we hereto subscribe our names.

In the issue of May 1980 there is a lengthy article, under the heading 'What hope for Protestants in Éire politics', devoted to emphasising the fact that although there are individual 'statutory' Protestants in politics in the Republic the chances of an 'ordinary' Protestant ever getting nominated, let alone elected, are nil.

Finally, in March 1981 the *Orange Standard* highlights the suggestion made by the Rev. John Knox, peace education officer of the Irish Council of Churches, that a civil rights movement may be needed for Protestants in the Irish Republic. The Rev. Mr Knox 'envisaged such a movement concerning itself with contraception, divorce and pressures put on partners in inter-church marriages'.

4
'Modernisation' and Northern Ireland

The importance of religion in the present situation in Northern
Ireland has been referred to throughout the previous chapters
of this book and has been dwelt upon at some length in the
last chapter. It will be referred to frequently throughout the
remainder of this work and is, in fact, the overriding concern
of this attempt at adding insights to the analysis of the
'problem' we are confronting in Northern Ireland. There is,
however, a need to avoid falling into the 'single-causal' trap
that has ensnared so many interpreters of the situation here
and which we have been at pains to avoid. We can no longer
talk of a simple 'Nationalist' argument or its more violent
expression in the 'Republican' answer to the case. If those
arguments were correct, then the problems they confront
could be solved through the operation of the political
institution in this society via negotiation between the elected
representatives of both sides. The facts indicate that this is
not possible. If we adopt the single-causal analysis of the
Marxist school, then all we have to do is to destroy the actual
structure of institutions which constitute the society of
Northern Ireland — and, incidentally, every other society in
the West — and start off from scratch. This is simple in
theory but might pose certain problems in practice, and the
prospect of enduring those problems might not really commend itself to the members of the society in question. By
the same token, we cannot say that religious belief is the
only causal factor in the situation — otherwise we would fall
into the same absurdity as the other explanations offer and
suggest that all Protestants become Roman Catholics or vice
versa.

We have to confront the fact that there is no single-causal

explanation of the troubles which plague the society encompassed in the State of Northern Ireland. If this is the case, then we must surely look for the elements which make up the total complex of issues that keep the population of that society deeply divided and that make hatred and distrust constant factors in its social life. All-embracing theories are helpful in the sense that they give us insights into the situation and provide us with questions to ask of it. But they are helpful only in that sense; they cannot 'explain' everything, because they look at 'everything' from one predetermined stance. Their focus determines their analysis, and the analysis itself becomes less valuable because it is determined by self-inflicted myopia. In this respect, the analyses produced by those who are in the broad, general tradition of the Marxist school are helpful in the sense that they draw our attention to the significance of the operation of the economic institution and its relationship with the political institution. The interplay of these two institutions is, of course, vital in any society, not just Northern Ireland; but they are not the sole sources from which human action springs and should not be treated as such. By the same token, the Nationalist and Republican interpretations of the situation, while equally as seductive as the Marxist in terms of 'whole' explanations, are based solely on an assumption that a particular political ideology is shared by the minority group and that that ideology dominates their lives and dictates their social action.[1] This approach is helpful in the sense that it highlights the fact that ideology *does* play a part in human action and that it must, therefore, be taken into account. It also proves, many times over, that the ideologies existing in the north of Ireland, amongst both groups, are not simply conditioned by economic and political expediency but have a life-generating force of their own. This explanation ceases to be helpful when it overlooks the fact that this 'ideology' may be rooted in a religiously inspired worldview which is not shared by the whole of the society and when it dismisses the opposing worldview as being externally imposed by the forces of an ill-defined 'imperialism'. It would have been more productive of understanding if the proponents of this line of analysis had widened their arguments to include *all* members of Northern Ireland's society. To do that, however, would have involved recognising the fact that Northern Ireland as a society actually exists and is not simply an appendage of the Republic of Ireland or of Britain. In this connection, while it is important to give due weight to the influence of these two countries on Northern Ireland, it is, nevertheless, necessary to accept the fact that there is a Northern Ireland society existing independently of both. Our understanding will be advanced only if we bear this *fact* in mind and treat Northern Ireland as a society in its own right, albeit a society small in numbers and subject to immense pressure from the two larger groups mentioned.

The proponents of the 'two-culture' argument come nearer to an understanding of Northern Ireland precisely because they *do* recognise the fact of its existence as a society. The problem here is that their claim that there are two cultures in the province is based on what is, by sociological standards, a woefully inadequate definition of 'culture'. Culture for them means an historical tradition which expresses itself mainly through the symbolic protection of an ancient language — Irish — and through various art forms, mainly poetry and drama, which express the 'native genius' of a particular branch of the Celtic people. It is also reflected in the sports and pastimes which are claimed to be the main preoccupation of one section of society and which are supposed to be particularly 'Irish' in origin. All of these features are subsumed in a 'national' identity which has its own symbolic expressions — flags, feast-days and the manner in which history is taught in the schools — and which is closely linked with a particular form of religious belief and the latter's organisational expression. This culture exists alongside another culture within the same society, and the result is that both are locked in mortal combat. This other 'culture' is identified by the same criteria as that applied to the 'Irish'. It expresses itself through a particular language — English — and it may have its own particular art forms. Its members engage in sports and pastimes that are British in origin and are the common pursuits of people 'across the water'. All of these features are also subsumed in a 'national' identity which has its own symbolic expressions and which is closely linked with a particular form of religious belief and organisation.[2]

This explanation has the added merit that it gives at least passing acknowledgment to the fact that religious belief is a part of a group's culture and that it can be the cause of friction between groups. It does not recognise the fact, however, that when we speak of a society's culture we are referring to a whole way of life and not just certain aspects of it. That way of life subsumes not just art forms and certain sports but also generally accepted patterns of work, standards of housing, levels of hygiene — both public and private — levels of income, priorities in expenditure of that income, methods of electing governments and the whole field of entertainment. That there are differences between sections of both the majority and minority groups in Northern Ireland in terms of political ideology cannot be denied. That there are substantial differences between both groups in terms of religious belief is evident. These are aspects of culture. But that on the whole range of other factors which have been mentioned as constituting culture there is a high degree of similarity between both groups is also self-evident. Protestants and Roman Catholics in Northern Ireland have a great deal in common in respect to those basic elements of culture. Even in the few areas where it is assumed that there is a major difference, the distinction between the two groups is not as clear as is often claimed. Although, for example, emphasis is put on the preservation of the Irish language, very few of the minority group speak it on a daily basis and English is accepted by both sections of society as their normal means of communication.[3] English is the language of the poetry and drama of creative artists from both groups; the themes differ according to the individual but the vehicle of expression remains the same. In terms of sports, while a substantial number of the Roman Catholic minority do, in fact, play 'Irish' games, a common interest is showed by both groups in the 'British' game which seems to dominate youthful minds — soccer. Finally, that dimension of culture known as 'popular' music prevails in popularity amongst both groups and provides a common ground of interest for Protestant and Roman Catholic alike. Under these circumstances, religious beliefs and the political ideology linked with them are becoming increasingly prominent in distinguishing the two groups. This is not something to be taken for granted. The process of social change which is highlighting those two aspects of culture and increasing their divisive effect in terms of violent conflict needs to be examined.

One of the concepts employed by sociologists to help in the analysis of social change is that of 'modernisation'. The concept is, if used properly, not meant as yet another overall explanation of complex phenomena but as a means of entry into the analysis of the operation of such phenomena and, as such, the beginnings of an understanding of them.[4] In general terms, 'modernisation' is the process within a society which marks the transition inside that society from a traditional folk form of structure to that of the complex social organisation associated with urban, industrialised societies. As the history of western societies demonstrates, the major instruments of modernisation are the development of industrialisation and the phenomenon closely linked with it, urbanisation. Industrialisation involves the growth of mass production, the development of heavy industries, the spread of factory work and the consequent destruction of old patterns of work and the creation of new ones. The industries have to be located in a centralised position where effective means of transportation can be efficiently developed so that materials can be easily moved into the manufacturing complex and the finished products moved out and distributed. A work force has to be readily available, located close to the industry and this in turn means that urbanisation takes place, involving a movement of people from rural areas into rapidly growing towns and cities. So, the society undergoes a change, in some cases a very rapid change, from one style of physical life located in rural surroundings and adjusted to that type of environment to another style located in an urban setting and having to adjust to that.

It is not, however, simply in one aspect of life that changes occur. Modernisation affects not only the economy but all the other major institutions in society, and changes take place in government, religion, education and social structure, including the structure of the family. This means that the whole culture of the society undergoes change and there are shifts and developments in knowledge, beliefs, values, self-conceptions and ways of life in general. The general tendency, under the pressure of modernisation, is towards uniformity of culture throughout the society in question. This involves an increase in the degree to which beliefs, values and tastes are shared by people of different groups and categories. This effect is produced by several factors all working together; they include the spread of formal education through a school system made available to all young members of the society and the resultant high degree of literacy and consequent access to one powerful branch of the mass media. The 'levelling' effect of this is increased by the ability to gain knowledge of members of other groups through increased mobility, both physical and social, which allows a wider identity of interest to develop among members of the same society. Mass production and mass markets, buttressed by skilful and sophisticated advertising techniques, have meant that patterns of consumption have become increasingly standardised. In this sense, also, ways of using leisure time and tastes in entertainment are becoming increasingly commonly shared by large sections of society under the pressure of the entertainment industry and the use the latter makes of the mass media, particularly radio and television. Finally, in order to be able to operate such a complex society efficiently, government has become more centralised, with means of communication made more efficient and effective.

In terms of its more profound effects on the lives of members of society — that is, on the norms and values they hold, modernisation is generally accepted as implying an increasing trend towards 'secularisation' and 'individualisation'. The concept of secularisation is a difficult one and the question of its application to contemporary urban society is hotly debated by sociologists (see below, Chapter 5, where it is considered in connection with the present situation in Northern Ireland). At the moment it is sufficient to consider it in its broadest sense as implying a shift in the bases on which people build their norms and values. This shift is from a 'sacred' base, founded on received doctrines, dogmas and traditions, to a 'secular' base founded on the principle of scepticism and the need to question all received wisdom. The change implies that most people in society no longer hold in unquestioning respect traditional patterns of norms and beliefs and the procedures and associations linked with them; they prefer, instead, to adopt rational and utilitarian attitudes which enable such traditions to be adjusted or changed to meet the exigencies of the moment. So, modern society is characterised by reliance on rationality rather than custom, by activism rather than fatalism and by an unquenchable desire for 'progress' rather than reverence for tradition. The latter characteristic expresses itself in particular in the sense that now we not only accept change but strongly desire it because we associate it, particularly in the sense of technological development, with progress.

'Individualisation' here is a shorthand term for the way in which modernisation is affecting the status a person holds in the society of which he or she is a member. In the past in 'simpler' societies the status a person held, and the roles associated with it, were defined by his membership in a particular family or tribe. He was a unit in a larger organisation and was not regarded as an individual in his own right. Hence, in the world of work, for example, he was given a job on the basis of kinship or friendship rather than on qualifications indicating merit or skill. Now, however, under the pressure of change, each individual is identified as a responsible member of society in his own right. The identity thus awarded to him is confirmed in the political field, for example, by giving him the *right* to take part on an equal footing with everyone else in the election of the government of the society of which he is a member. Because he has rights, however, he also has responsibilities to himself and to others and is accountable for his own actions. He is employed on the basis of merit and qualification, and much of his daily life is taken up by work through which he seeks reward and gains recognition from his fellow members of society. So, our societies are conceived of as being composed of individuals, relating closely to each other on the basis of recognition of

mutual rights and responsibilities, and not of closely constructed kinship groups relating to each other on a 'bargain-
ing' basis.

Finally, modernisation has a continuing impact on the
general structure of the society it is affecting. This is seen,
for example, in the increasing size of this society's political
and economic units. Government sets up centralised structures
through which it can increase control and influence over
the lives if the citizens; the structures themselves become
more formal and rational, more 'bureaucratic'. Industry and
commerce form themselves into larger and larger groups in
order to increase efficiency, maximise production and reap
higher profits. At the same time the major institutions in
society become more specialised in their operations as do
the people whose daily activity forms those institutions.
Given the breakdown of the old social groups, social contacts
become more varied and the number of relationships we, as
individuals, have to enter, greater. As a result, the 'class'
system in many societies tends to become more fluid and
open and less easy to define. All in all, then, a society undergoing the process of modernisation finds that its whole
system is becoming more complex and its parts more inter-
dependent.

It is important to remember, however, in connection with
the process of modernisation that although it affects all the
institutions in society it does not do so uniformly. That is,
the process of change may take place more rapidly in one
institution than it does in another. To use a simile, modernisation is not like a 'wave' which strikes all institutions
together, carrying away the superstructure and leaving behind
a foundation on which they all build anew at the same rate.
It is more like a series of wavelets which rapidly overwhelm
some institutions but only weaken the bases of others. So
that change in the economy of a society may proceed very
rapidly, while change in its political institution is much slower
and change in religion slower still. This consideration produced
Ogburn's well-known concept of 'cultural lag' whereby the
culture of a society is put under some degree of stress
because the institution, for example, of the family is not
changing at a rate sufficient to allow its members to cope

with the change in the economy. Patterns of work that were based on the needs of a rural society, which related closely to patterns of family relationships, built upon an extended kinship network which produced the type of mutual co-operation needed to deal with the economic exigencies of life. With the transition from a rural to an urban economy the pattern of work changed and the support of the extended family no longer became so significant in the economic sense. But the family structure had not only provided economic support, it had also supplied the basis for a great deal of personal relationships. Its importance for its members was not restricted to the material things of life but was significant for the emotional well-being of those members, and 'family loyalty' was the basis of many of the values which influenced their lives. With the economic foundation of the family now gone, the members were left with the problem of maintaining the other relationships, so vital to their needs, in the face of an increasingly hostile social environment. Strenuous efforts have, in fact, been made in many modernised societies to retain those relationships but the 'family circle' has tended to become increasingly narrow, and its significance as a source of values has diminished steadily as the family institution adjusts itself to the changes in the other institutions. In a personal and vital sense, then, the process of modernisation because of its unevenness puts great stress on the members of the society in which that process is taking place. This is true of all societies but is particularly significant for Northern Ireland where, it will be maintained, the wavelets of modernisation have submerged some institutions but have lapped unavailingly at others, particularly the religious.

Northern Ireland, as a society, has been subjected to that process of social change summarised as modernisation, in the same way that other societies have. The *manner* in which this process has taken place is, of course, unique to Northern Ireland as it is to any other society; the *pace* of change is also different from its near neighbours — slower in certain respects than in mainland Britain and faster than in the Irish Republic. This is not the place to rehearse the social history of Northern Ireland in the twentieth century but some attention needs to be paid to the major factors of change that are influencing the present situation. Those factors are conditioned by the situation that the economy of Northern Ireland and its political structure are dependent to some extent on the influence of other societies. This point has been made on a number of occasions throughout this work and should not need to be laboured further. It is not this dependence which makes Northern Ireland a special case for consideration; there are many other societies in the contemporary world whose economy could not exist without the support of outside investment and the influence which this support implies. Their internal social structure is affected by this relationship to some extent, but it is not entirely dependent upon it. In this respect Northern Ireland is affected by Britain and the Republic of Ireland but is not entirely re-structured by the influence of either of these societies. It is necessary again to state that we must treat Northern Ireland as a society in its own right, if we are to approach an understanding of it, and not just as an appendage of Britain or that part of Ireland artificially separated from the remaining twenty-six counties.

Northern Ireland experienced a degree of modernisation in the economic sense during the period when industrialisation and urbanisation were developing rapidly in Britain generally, that is, during the late eighteenth, nineteenth and early twentieth centuries. Some attention has already been paid, in Chapter 1, to the growth of Belfast during that period and the impact that this urbanisation had on the relationships between the two religious groups. Because of the development of the industries in the city — shipbuilding, linen, engineering — and because of the fact that it was a port and so had a natural means of communication with the outside world and an efficient way of distributing its products, Belfast acted as a magnet in terms of drawing population from the surrounding rural areas. The movement of people, common to the rest of Britain, from the countryside to the town took place in what is now Northern Ireland. Thus, the economic and social structure of the society began to be modernised in the same way as the parallel structures of many other societies in the West. There is, however, an important difference between Northern Ireland and mainland

Britain in this respect. It is estimated that at the present time (1981), approximately 60 per cent of the total population of Northern Ireland live either in Belfast itself or within a thirty-mile radius of the city. It may thus be claimed that a majority of the citizens are urbanised and that the 'problem' of Northern Ireland may be regarded as the problem of Belfast. The statistic, however, needs to be looked at in a broader context if its significance is to be fully appreciated. Thirty miles may seem a short distance to an observer who is used to thinking in terms of huge conurbations within which people commute sometimes twice that number of miles per day in order to get back and forth to work. This amount of travelling helps to constitute a style of life and an attitude towards it which is characteristic of the urban dweller in many of the large cities of Europe and the United States. The question of physical distance, however, is one of scale, and the scale by which individuals judge that distance is related to all sorts of other considerations rooted in their physical and social environment. Thirty miles may not seem too long a travelling distance to people who live in the dormitory suburbs of London, Paris, New York or Chicago and who identify themselves with those cities. In Northern Ireland, on the other hand, a journey of thirty miles in any direction from Belfast will take you almost one third of the way across the entire province and into a style of life very different from that associated with urban living. To quote, in this connection, one example, may help to illustrate the point being made. The New University of Ulster is located close to the town of Coleraine — population 14,000 — and within six miles of two other towns, Portstewart and Portrush, both with populations of less than 8,000 people. The combination of these three towns is known as the Triangle, with Coleraine being the commercial and industrial nexus of the life of the area. Portrush and Portstewart are both located on the northern coast of Northern Ireland and are seaside resorts, making a substantial proportion of their living from summer visitors who now, because of the 'troubles', tend to come mainly from within Northern Ireland. In the scale of 'distance', Belfast is remote from the Triangle; the residents of the latter are proud of

Belfast in the sense that it is their capital city, has a 'sophisticated' way of life and has good stores to be visited on their
occasional shopping trips. By the same token, the Triangle
is as remote from the citizens of Belfast as Miami is from
Chicago or the Costa Brava is from London.

It is here that the whole question of physical distance and
its significance in the lives of people and the scale by which
they measure it comes into play. The Triangle is remote from
Belfast in many ways which affect the lives of its people: in
physical terms it is, in fact, just over fifty miles from the
city. This needs to be taken into account when we are
dealing with the statistic which shows that almost two
thirds of the population of Northern Ireland live within
thirty miles of Belfast. The implication of this raw figure is
that these people may be treated as 'urbanised', and therefore 'typical' of Northern Ireland society. They cannot be.
They may just as well be three hundred or three thousand
miles away from Belfast, depending upon the scale which
the observer is using and imposing upon the social reality of
Northern Ireland.

Even if this figure were correct in terms of a simple
measurement of the workings of the social structure, it still
tells us little of value about Northern Ireland's society. The
only other city in Northern Ireland is Derry, which has a
population of less than 60,000. This population does not
exactly constitute a massive conurbation, by any standards;
in Europe or the United States it would be regarded as a large
village with pretensions to becoming a town, with its title
of 'city' reflecting a historical tradition rather than a demographic reality. This is not to say that historical tradition is
of less importance than demographic size in influencing the
world view of the inhabitants of a particular location. It is,
in fact, saying something different — that is, that there are
influences other than the size or density of the population
which influence the actions of the population involved.

Outside of Belfast and Derry the remainder of the population of Northern Ireland live in small towns or villages where
the prevailing social influence is rural rather than urban. The
lives of these people still are influenced by the factors which
prevail in a pre-modernised environment and this means that

their attitudes and values still owe something to the sacred and the corporate rather than to the secular and individualistic. The influence of tradition is still strong among them and the received wisdom from that tradition still powerful in affecting their lives and motivations. Kinship ties are still effective in this society to an extent far beyond that of other, more modernised societies, including that of mainland Britain, and commitment to those ties, including loyalty to the traditions treasured by the 'family' is still very strong. This situation allows the survival of phenomena in terms of political attitudes and ideology which seem 'strange' to outside observers and add to the bewilderment of the people who feel obliged to provide solutions to the problem of Northern Ireland. In terms of this society the power of old beliefs and attitudes still expresses itself through the structures of society which impinge most closely upon the lives of its individual members and which motivated them first to build and now to continue to support the associations which articulate those beliefs and traditions in a political sense — Unionism and the Orange Order on the one hand, and nationalism and the Roman Catholic clerical structure on the other.

The society of Northern Ireland developed on the basis of two groups of people moulded in their own traditions and encapsulated in a political structure which forced them to continue living together and to construct a society in which they could both survive and prosper. For many years that society was static, trapped into a state of frozen immobility, mainly through the operation of politico-religious influences. The wavelets of modernisation had hit the economic institution but had simply swirled around the religious and political institutions of Northern Ireland. The latter were suspended in time and impervious to change, mainly through the efforts of the Unionist party and the Orange Order on the one hand, and the Nationalist/Republican elements and the Roman Catholic clergy on the other. Conflicts occurred between the two groups but the Unionist/Protestant majority were able to maintain control by adopting, through their governments at Stormont, a basically defensive atttitude to government and a single policy — that

of maintaining the union. For a long period after 1920, therefore, Northern Ireland could be regarded as a basically stable
society; but it was stable because it was static.

Changes began to develop after 1945 as a result of a
further degree of modernisation in the economic institution.
In the immediate post-World War Two period, Northern
Ireland experienced some years of unparalleled prosperity
during which both the standard of living of its people and
their level of expectations rose well above those of the 1930s.
At the same time, the social welfare legislation introduced by
the post-war British governments was applied to Northern
Ireland and the new economic prosperity was now under-
pinned by a structure of health, welfare and employment
benefits which ensured that there could be no return to the
poverty and hardship of the 1930s. There were crucial
changes also in education, the most significant being that
of free access of university education for those who could
pass the necessary examinations.

All these changes benefited both sections of the population, of course, but their impact was greater on the Roman
Catholic minority than on the Protestant majority largely
because the former had more leeway to make up than the
latter. In particular, the more open access to university education was taken advantage of by the Roman Catholics and
substantial numbers of this group began to enter higher
education in the late 1940s and 1950s. This process has
continued for the last thirty years, until now, although no
precise statistics are available, the impression is that Roman
Catholic students constitute a higher proportion of the
university population than their proportion of the total
population would indicate as likely. The result is that we are
now witnessing the emergence of a new phenomenon in
Northern Ireland — a Roman Catholic middle class with a
leadership drawn from the highly educated and articulate
minority who were the first to benefit from the university
education which became available in the immediate post-
war years.[5]

This change in the social class structure amongst the
minority group has been accompanied by some degree
of change also in the aspirations of that group. There has

been a movement away, for instance, from support for the old 'Nationalist' and 'Republican' parties because their policies were not now answering the needs of those members of the minority group whose aspirations to and expectations of the standard of life they were now able to hope for had been raised by their education and training. The single-plank policies of a united Ireland appealed less and less to such people. Unification was not their top priority; it was, and is, becoming increasingly irrelevant to their lives. They wanted, instead, social reform and the opening-up of the society in which they lived, to enable them to achieve the standard of life they wanted and to share in the government of that society.

This new development is fragile and subject to shifts engendered by current events — as one would expect of such a relatively recent phenomenon. There is, for example, a current decline in the fortunes of the Alliance party, brought about probably by the emotions aroused among Roman Catholics by the H Block campaign and the consequent increased polarisation of the two religious groups. It is, however, impossible to say whether this particular develop- ment marks a long-term trend. It is more likely to be a further fluctuation in the process mentioned and to have little long-term significance. It may also be that the Alliance party, for all its merits, does not adequately represent the views of the new Roman Catholic stratum in society. This new leadership of the Roman Catholic minority was begin- ning to see, by the 1960s, that their major interests lay in establishing their position within a new *Northern Ireland* society and in achieving the formation of a political institution which would give them a say in directing that society. Hence, the decade of the sixties saw a new political phenomenon in Northern Ireland. This took the form of a campaign *not* for removal of the border and the end of partition within Northern Ireland but for the re-structuring of Northern Ireland's society itself to allow equality of opportunity for all the members of that society. The Civil Rights campaign — which is what I am talking about — was significant in many ways, not least of which was that by the very fact of its existence it recognised the reality of Northern

Ireland's society. It was a campaign not to abolish Northern Ireland but to reform it; and it was led by Roman Catholics from the new group we have referred to who managed to work, for a time at least, with Protestants who had shared in their educational and social experiences.

These developments caused consternation among the Protestant majority in the North and provoked the reaction which has played a vital role in the continuing turbulence affecting this society. The reasons for both the reaction and the prolonged violence will be looked at in the concluding chapters of this work, at some length. Some points, however, should be made here. The concept of 'modernisation' is too wide in its implications to be used for a close analysis of what is producing the present situation in Northern Ireland. It is, nevertheless, a useful explanatory context into which to fit such an analysis. There is a sense in which the society of Northern Ireland is undergoing severe stress precisely because of the processes acting upon it that are associated with modernisation, and this stress, in turn, provides the background for the sharp degree of *violent* conflict taking place in the province. In Shils's terms, the Roman Catholic minority is beginning to move from the 'periphery' to the 'centre' of the society, and this movement is producing shock waves which are reverberating throughout the whole of Northern Ireland. The reason for this is to be found in one of the characteristics of the process of modernisation mentioned earlier: as a process it proceeds unevenly. In the case of Northern Ireland, this unevenness is demonstrated in its effects on three institutions — the economic, the political and the religious. The impact of modernisation on the economy has been substantial, though not comprehensive, and it is this impact which has brought about the changing social status of the minority group and increased and modified the aspirations of that group.

At the same time, the process of modernisation has had very little impact on the political institution and almost none on the religious. But change in one institution in society has to have some effect on all other institutions, even if that effect is only to produce violent reaction from them, and, in this way, to show how deeply entrenched their interests are and how strongly their integrity will be defended. What the factors producing modernisation in Northern Ireland have succeeded in doing is to bring about change in the economy, and at the same time, to throw into sharp focus the deeply divisive elements in the society. Those elements have been there for a long time but their destructive force was contained as long as the society was static and not subjected to the pressures of change. Once these pressures began to be felt, the power of such elements to resist change and provoke conflict began once again to come into action. So that, while differences in the social structure between Protestants and Roman Catholics are being slowly eliminated, the importance of the other difference — religion — is being increasingly emphasised. Conflict now centres upon the distinction of religious belief and the world view based upon it.

5
Is Religion Declining in Importance?

From the religious point of view, humanity has entered
a long night that will become darker with the passing of the
generations, and of which no end can yet be seen. It is a
night in which there seems to be no place for a conception
of God, or for a sense of the sacred, and ancient ways of
giving significance to our own existence, of confronting life
and death, are becoming increasingly untenable. At bottom,
the motivations for religious behaviour and for faith persist
— the need to explain ourselves and what surrounds us, the
anguish, and the sense of precariousness. But man remains
uncertain whether somewhere there exists, or ever existed,
something different from uncertainty, doubt, and existential
insecurity.

S. S. Acquaviva,
*The Decline of the Sacred
in Industrial Society* (1979)
pp. 201-2.

What we are predicting, then, is that in the next thirty to
fifty — even a hundred — years we will not witness the
rapid, or even the gradual evolution, but rather the slow
evolution of religion. Of course it is possible that the whole
process of human history has been so shaken in the last
century that the projection of trends in the future, on the
basis of the past and the present, is no longer valid. It may
be that one can no longer assert that just as religion has
evolved into the present, so it will continue to evolve into
the future, perhaps at an accelerated rate. Furthermore,
even though religion has outlived all those who prophesied
its doom in the past, it may be that the human condition
has changed so much that this time the prophets of doom
are correct.

But the assertion that gradual evolution is being replaced
by evolutionary doom must be made on the basis of poetic
insight or metaphysical abstraction, or, quite possibly,
revelation. Nothing in the data or the theories of

behavioral science enables the sociologist to cope adequately with propositions made on the data from poetry, metaphysics, or access to the plans of the Deity. All he can reply to such arguments is to observe that we will just have to wait and see. . . .

A. M. Greeley,
Religion in the Year 2000 (1969)
pp. 174-5.

In deliberating on *what* shall be done — our social policies — and *how* it shall be done — our social organization and techniques — modern society has given up the precedents and the lessons of the past, as no longer relevant and, in consequence, the role and place of religion in society has been severely disrupted. The future orientation of modern man has affected both the institutions of faith — the Churches — and the content of the faith of the ordinary man.

All the evidence from our times suggests that, at least in the western world, the Christian faith is in serious decline. What is true of the institutions of the Church appears also to be true of the belief and practice of the majority of men. Religion, particularly in its traditional form, has become socially less and less significant. Most modern men, for most of their time, in most of their activities, are very little touched — if they are touched at all — by any direct religious intimations. Even those who count themselves as believers, who subscribe to the tenets of a church, and who attend services regularly, nevertheless operate in social space in which beliefs about the supernatural are rendered in part irrelevant.

B. Wilson,
Contemporary Transformations of Religion (1979)
pp. 5-6.

These three extracts have been quoted to demonstrate some of the different approaches that sociologists now take to the question of the survival of religion in modern society. The excerpts have been taken from the work of some of the major scholars who are addressing the problem now. There are more (see Notes and Bibliography). These have been chosen because they represent three trends of analysis all based on a close examination of the data which exist relating to belief in religion and the practice of that belief.

Acquaviva, in his reflections on the state of religion in contemporary society, portrays human beings as being locked into a desperate and desolate struggle to comprehend the reality of their existence when they have no certainty, in terms of received wisdom, upon which to base beliefs that will help to guide them. He concludes, on a note of gentle melancholy, that perhaps the present condition and future fate of mankind is to continue in doubt and struggle. But he leaves the question open. Greeley, on the other hand, calls upon the evidence of the present to show that religion, in its institutionalised forms, is changing and evolving and he does not forecast a long dark night for mankind. He buttresses his arguments with appeals to the history of the survival of religion, which survival allows him to engage in the irony of the first paragraph quoted. His conclusion is, in contrast to Acquaviva's, one of hope, but again the question is left open — 'we will just have to wait and see. . .'. Greeley and Acquaviva may differ from each other in terms of the emphasis they place upon their conclusions but each has a respect for the non-measurable elements in human action and thus a regard for the humility with which the sociologist, like any other scholar, should address the task of interpreting the complex of perceived information which he is attempting to analyse. Wilson is less inhibited and is confident enough to make statements like '. . . the Christian faith is in serious decline . . . Religion, particularly in its traditional form, has become socially less and less significant.' His analysis is of a much higher order of sophistication than the Marxist analysis already referred to above; he is not trying to 'dissolve' religion as a factor in social action but rather to explain its increasing insignificance. Nevertheless, this is a remarkably confident statement about a very delicate problem — the relationship between religious belief, its institutionalised form and the daily actions of members of a society. It was not made in connection with Northern Ireland but, given the implicit universality of his statements, it should be possible to apply it to Northern Ireland. This would, I think, be very difficult to do.[1]

Of the three approaches, Greeley's, with his emphasis on evolution and change, is the most productive of understanding. A major problem exists in the type of analysis put forward not only by Wilson but by other scholars who adopt his line of approach: implicit in their arguments is the assumption that the development of human societies and, therefore, of the institutions, like religion, that encapsulate the actions and motivations of the members of those societies, proceeds in a linear fashion. This means that institutions take part in a progressive line of development which results in either their emergence into a state of full fruition or their ultimate disappearance. In the case of the institution of religion, the assumption behind this argument is that religion was once important but, under the impact of the development of other major institutions in society — a development which implies an increasing 'rationalisation' of human action — it is becoming progressively less so and will eventually disappear. Religion will 'wither away', just as, in Marxist terms, that other institution — the State — will wither away when human nature eventually ceases to be alienated from itself through actions of the political and economic institutions in society.[2]

The ideology which lies behind this line of argument is based upon an analysis of history which sees it as a constant progression towards the ultimate realisation of the nature of 'man', a realisation in which religion can play no part. The operation of the institution of religion, then, is seen as declining in a progressive way from the time when it was of great importance in the lives of individuals to the time when it will eventually cease to be of any real significance at all in motivating human action. To put it crudely, there was a time when 'people' were religious but that religiosity is progressively becoming less important as society moves in its linear track towards its ultimate, rational millennium.[3]

The argument is persuasive, if we accept that society does 'progress' in this way and does not, in fact, double back on itself. If the latter happens, then we cannot simply speak of a progressive decline in any institution; we can only say that in certain periods of time and in certain societies those institutions are of lesser or greater importance in relation to the others.[4] And that their decline in one period does not necessarily indicate that they are on the way to extinction. It may simply be that they are appearing in a different form, a form which responds to the demands and pressures of the social environment on the one hand, and puts its stamp, as Weber would say, on this social environment on the other. The history of the family as an institution is demonstrative of this. We are accustomed to the public utterances of people who see a decline in something called 'family life' and who are prepared either to deplore or to welcome this as a phenomenon. Yet all the data available to us, whether historical, sociological or anthropological, demonstrate that while the family may vary in shape or form and its functions change according to the society in which it is implanted, nevertheless the family as a unit has existed and still exists in all known societies. Though its functions may increase or decline, the family demonstrably is not on a linear path to destruction; as society changes, it changes and continues to emerge if not triumphant at least still there. It may be bloody but it is still unbowed.

The survival of this one vital institution in society is quoted in order to demonstrate the fact that we cannot adopt a simple one-dimensional view of the history of human societies, and attempt to demonstrate, on the basis of that view, that any of its institutions is doomed to extinction. This applies particularly, in our case, to religion. It may be that institutionalised forms of religion have varied from century to century and from society to society. It may well be, also, that the prominence that those institutionalised forms took in directing the lives of members of society has risen or declined during the passage of those centuries. We may well agree, finally, with Wilson and say that in the western world religion has become socially less significant.[5] But it has become less significant at this particular time and in certain societies only. The fact that this has happened should not blind us to the fact that in some societies religion still has an institutional significance which gives it an immense importance. Northern Ireland is a case in point. Part of the reason why the 'problem' here is not understood and apparently is impenetrable of analysis, is this blindness to the fact of the importance of religion. We have convinced ourselves that religion is not important in Western European societies and that, therefore, it cannot and *should not* be

important in Northern Ireland and cannot *really* be contributing to the violent conflict here. This, at best, is an over-
simplified view of the state of the society under examination.
It would not, I think, commend itself to the majority of
the population of Northern Ireland.

In our earlier discussion of modernisation and the effect this
process has on societies, we briefly referred to the factor of
'specialisation'; institutions become more specialised in their
functions, under the influence of modernisation, and so,
consequently, do the actions of the human beings who make
up those institutions. The implications of this need to be
briefly explored in connection with the effect that this
specialisation has upon religion, its practice and organisation.
The simplest expression of the application of this approach
to religion is to be found, again, in the linear view of the
evolution of society. In the beginning society existed in, by
our terms, a primitive state wherein the functions now
performed by the political, economic, educational and
familial institutions were in fact carried out by one institution
which controlled the operations of that society. This
institution combined the political and economic functions
necessary to run the society and was supported by an
extensive family and kinship network which helped to
spread, amongst its members, the attitudes and values
necessary to ensure that the social group survived, prospered
and gave its allegiance to the persons who led it. It was also
supported by the operation of religious belief which provided
the received wisdom upon which all members of society
based their daily actions and which enabled them, in
Durkheim's terms, to live together in a state of solidarity.
In such societies there was, then, a state of 'religiousness'
which was diffused throughout the social structure and which
pervaded every aspect of the lives of its people. Under these
circumstances, religion must be awarded a very high status in
the list of priorities which determine the action of human
beings because it is everywhere present in their lives and
operates as a constant point of reference by which they can
judge their actions. More than this, it provides a standard
whereby the actions of others can be judged and, consequently,

a set of norms to which all are expected to adhere. Religion, then, in these societies is of prime importance and must be treated as such.

The position changes, however, with the passage of centuries and the effect this has upon the internal structure of societies. As societies endure the process of history they adjust to its demands. These demands express themselves in forms which make it no longer possible for one institution to control the destinies of the folk who make the society; the simple structure, and the infrastructure which supports it, become unsuited to the needs of the people whose lives it once served. There is now, in a complex world, a need to develop institutions that can cope with the exigencies of the situation they must confront. The answer is 'specialisation' — specialisation in all forms of life. The society develops a specialised economic institution to deal with the exploitation of the natural resources of the physical environment, to maximise the production from that environment and to make the distribution as efficient and satisfying as possible, both to producers and to consumers. A separate political institution is also developed because the government of the society has become so complex that it demands the full-time attention of a proportion of its members who are prepared to undertake the responsibilities and accept the rewards that come from directing the affairs of their fellow members. Education now can no longer be left to the haphazard and possibly capricious influence of the kinship network; it has to be organised and directed in order to serve the good purposes of the society — the economy needs a labour force and the government needs to be composed of people who have been trained to articulate the demands of the folk they represent. Education, then, needs to be carefully structured and so a formal apparatus is erected which will meet the needs of the society and enable it to cope with the demands made upon it. The family also is re-structured; it no longer needs to be looked upon as a source of support for the other institutions in the sense that it once was. Its economic, political and educational functions are now no longer of prime importance; they are subsumed in the operations of the other institutions which have come into being and whose special purpose is to take care of the problems encountered in those areas. So, we have the birth of the 'nuclear' or 'conjugal' family consisting of husband, wife and children. This combination exists as a unit in its own right, with minimal contacts now with the kin of either husband or wife and, consequently, very little influence of that kin upon the children. The purpose of the family unit is now also special — it exists to provide mutual support, in an emotional sense, for its members. It is the one sure reference point in our lives in terms of a haven to retreat to in times of stress and a source of comfort when we find that coping with the demands of our highly compartmentalised life becomes too much for us.

Society, then, is moving through stages which result in the increasing differentiation of the institutions which express the lives of its members, with consequent specialisation. What happens, in this process, to religion? At one point in time, before this process started, it pervaded the entire structure of society. But now it has followed along the path taken by the other major institutions and become specialised. This is surely a logical progression. If the economy, government, education and the family assume particular tasks and thus become highly differentiated from each other, then one can expect the same of religion. And, sure enough, this is what happens. Religion assumes a specialised social role. It develops its own organisation — what we now call 'churches' — which visibly takes its place alongside the organisations of the other institutions. A set of beliefs which once were diffused throughout the whole of society are now encapsulated in a structure which forms just one section of a highly complex society. Religion, and, by definition, religious beliefs, are now 'specialised' and occupy a strictly compartmentalised position in the social system in which human beings live.

So, the process determined by the iron law of linear progression grinds on. The societies which form the context in which we all as human beings live are becoming increasingly complex and the result of this is that our lives are becoming increasingly compartmentalised. We live our lives, according to this law, as political man when we vote, as economic man when we earn the material means to survive, as educational man when we move through whatever cultural system our society devises and as family man when we need to relax from the exertions involved with coping with our other roles and look for the sympathy and support which is now the major characteristic of the family. In this sense, the major institutions of society change and evolve. They do not disappear; they simply change the form in which they represent themselves in society. Not so with religion. This is the one institution in society which, according to the proponents of the 'linear development' analysis of society, cannot survive. Although religion once was a very powerful, perhaps the most powerful, motivating force in social existence, and although, like the other institutions, it has adapted itself to the changing situations experienced by society, it cannot persist as the others have done. This is because, while the other institutions are essential to our lives, religion is not. Religious belief is 'a non-essential dimension of the human condition'[6] and, as such, cannot be regarded as even providing a trickle into the mainstream of human action. It is totally dependent upon the operation of the other institutions in society and is the product of social dynamics. In our complex, highly specialised societies religious belief becomes increasingly the private concern of individuals and does not impinge upon the life of society as a whole in any meaningful way.

Although this view is hotly debated by sociologists nowadays, it is powerfully argued, persuasive and therefore very influential. If you see this view in the context of a society like England, where decline in church membership and church attendance has been substantial and progressive since about the turn of the century and where it is not apparent that religion impinges to any significant degree on the lives of the people, then it is easy to see why an observer would not take the importance of religion very seriously.[7] Such observers then transfer this focus to Northern Ireland and attempt to analyse the social situation here on the same basis, assuming that religion here occupies a very low place on people's order of priorities. As a result, they are bewildered by the intensity of the conflict and the ferocity with which that conflict expresses itself.

The force of modernisation has had an uneven impact on the institutions of Northern Ireland. It has made a major impression on the economy, even though large sections of the province still remain relatively untouched by the factors of urbanisation and industrialisation, and the social class structure is undergoing change and development. It has affected education in the sense that a specialist institution has been developed here, consisting of a school and college structure very similar to that of the rest of the United Kingdom. The major difference, of course, is that in Northern Ireland there are effectively two educational systems, replicating each other and rigidly divided on religious grounds. On the one hand there is the system controlled by the Roman Catholic Church, through which all Roman Catholic children are supposed to proceed, and on the other hand there is the State system which is effectively Protestant. The data that exist indicate that the segregation between the two is virtually complete.[8] Only a tiny minority of Roman Catholic children go to State schools, and vice versa. In this sense, although the education has been modernised it has been modernised in a very peculiar way; and the result of this, ironically, has been to make the barrier between the majority and minority groups more rigid. It is only in the sectors of further and higher education that the Protestant and Catholic elements in the student population become integrated, and even here there is still some degree of segregation. This is in the field of teacher education where, although there is now a degree of integration in the universities, the Roman Catholic authorities still maintain two colleges exclusively for their own trainee teachers and a third college in the province has become identified as 'Protestant'.

In politics, modernisation has made very little impact. The operation of the political institution here still rotates around religious considerations. Although attempts have been made and are being made to form 'cross-sectarian' parties with social and economic issues their top priorities — as they would be in the rest of the United Kingdom — very little progress has been made in this direction. There is still no such thing as normal politics in Northern Ireland, 'normal', that is, in the sense that they are concentrated upon the material concerns which preoccupy most societies in the West.

Religion is the one institution which most successfully resisted change. It has not gone through the process outlined in the previous pages, carrying out a progressively more restricted role in the functioning of society. It has not become privatised and retreated into the depths of the personal lives of individuals. On the contrary, it still pervades this society in the sense that it was assumed to have pervaded all societies 'in the past'. In this respect, differences in religious belief between the majority and minority groups within Northern Ireland provide an immense, perhaps insurmountable, obstacle to the 'successful' completion of the modernising process and therefore to the development of a society which can be regarded as akin to the remainder of the United Kingdom, and judged on the basis of the criteria normally applied to western societies. Religious belief has a profound influence in Northern Ireland society and, as a result, *differences* in religious belief are of major social significance. At the present time these differences run too deeply and are too profound to be overcome by the forces of increasing prosperity and social mobility. It has already been pointed out that Northern Ireland experienced a period of unparalleled economic prosperity in the immediate post-war years and that this, coupled with the impact of social welfare reforms, helped to produce a period of comparative calm and the growth of hope and optimism for the future. It seemed as if relationships between the two groups had never been better and that the levelling out which was occurring in the economic sphere would bring about a greater degree of mutual understanding, respect and therefore sympathy between Protestant and Roman Catholic. The hope and optimism proved to be spurious.

These considerations will be returned to in the final chapter of this work, but a few points need to be made here. It can be argued, I think, that the economic forces operating in the post-war years had an unlooked-for side effect. These forces, by helping to diminish the social differences between

Protestants and Roman Catholics through the social structure, threw into greater relief the major ground of difference between the two groups — religion. As the other differences became obscured this difference became clearer. In this respect, the changes in the economic sphere accentuated the significance of religion in that they brought it more to the fore. They had the most disturbing effect on the Protestants, whose role in the conflict now became crucial. The new forces of social change threatened the old Protestant domin- ation of the State as Roman Catholics were brought on to a more equal footing with them. The movement of Roman Catholics from the periphery of Northern Ireland's society towards its centre meant changes in the structure of that society; it was no longer static and therefore controllable, as it had been for so many years after 1921. This called forth the atavistic fears of Protestants; if the changes were allowed to develop too far, then the State which was set up to protect the integrity of their belief system might break down and so their whole life-style be in serious danger of being destroyed by an aggressive Roman Catholicism. In this way, religion and the world view based upon it, particularly the political expression of that world view, became more sharply identified as the point of difference between the two groups as other differences faded in significance.

6
Towards a Sociological Analysis of Northern Ireland Society

We have dwelt at some length in the preceding chapters of this work on the factors producing conflict in Northern Ireland's society. These factors include historical tradition, which affects the two groups in the society in various ways and helps to produce ideological stances which are different and conflicting; and also the political institution, which reflects those ideological stances and operates to impose the will of one group upon the other; and religious belief which, at one and the same time, both influences the received wisdom of the historical tradition and underpins both the ideology and the political institutions which express it. Northern Ireland has existed in this situation since the State was established in 1920, and Ulster itself for many years before that. There has thus always been the potential for violent conflict here and that conflict has erupted on a number of occasions since 1921. What, then, is so different about the present situation?

The answer to that question lies mainly in the length of the present outbreak. It is by far the longest period of sustained violence in the history of Northern Ireland since its foundation as a state. It has already lasted twelve years and shows no signs of diminishing, and has produced an appalling cost in terms of human life and property. In those twelve years more than two thousand people have died as a direct result of the civil war taking place here and more than ten times that number have been injured and will consequently have a permanent reminder of this period all their lives. To get a perspective on this we will need to make some comparisons with other societies. Raw figures on their own do not tell us too much about social life — we need a standard against which to judge them so that their impact and meaning may become more real to us. We are constantly reminded, for example, that the gross number of people murdered in some major American cities exceeds in three years the total killed in Northern Ireland in twelve years. The purpose of this comparison is not clear, unless perhaps it is meant to imply that America is a more violent society than Northern Ireland. This is grossly misleading. A truer comparison would be to take the proportions of the total population involved and compare them on that basis; doing this indicates that between 1969 and 1981, 282,000 people would have been killed in the United States and more than two million injured in 'civil disturbances' if that society had gone through the same experiences as Northern Ireland. The comparable figures for the United Kingdom are over 75,000 people killed and more than three quarters of a million injured. This as a result not of war with outside powers but of conflict within the society itself. How could the societies of either of these major nations have coped with a human disaster on this scale? Would their social institutions have remained intact under such pressure or would they have disintegrated? The questions are unanswerable because the situation is unimaginable; the societies concerned have developed to a stage of social organisation and consensus about norms and values which make civil strife on this scale inconceivable.

This is what is of special significance in terms of the present violence in Northern Ireland. Its length and intensity make it unique. Previous outbreaks were relatively short-lived and capable of being contained within certain limits, even if those limits implied a degree of bloodshed which would be totally unacceptable in other societies. While many people suffered, the structure of the society itself was not, in the last resort, seriously threatened. The whole structure of the society of Northern Ireland is now under threat from the combination of a variety of forces working within it. The sociological problem is to attempt to identify those forces and to try to estimate why they should have made such an impact in the last two decades that they have not only produced, up to now, twelve years of violence and death but also seem likely to bring about irreversible changes in Northern Ireland society.

The interpretations based on the analyses examined earlier, that is the Nationalist, Republican, two-culture and Marxist, are not of great help in this regard. They either place too much emphasis on a single-causal analysis, as in the case of the first two, or are incomplete, as in the case of the third, or rely too much on ideological assumptions, as with the fourth. We would not want to prepare an alternative model so as to 'explain' the entire situation in Northern Ireland, but to help in some understanding of that situation and the forces acting upon it.

The evidence already referred to throughout this work indicates that Northern Ireland is undergoing a process of internal change which is, by its standards, proceeding at a rapid rate. The change is affecting the economic and social structure of the society, is impinging upon the political and having very little effect upon the religious. As a result of this uneven effect that these developments are having on its institutions, the society of Northern Ireland is being subjected to very severe stress which is producing internal conflict escalating into violence. In general terms, the change which is taking place here is from a relatively stable society composed of two groups distinguishable from each other in terms of religion, politics, and some features of cultural tradition, to a society where the two groups are mixing at a variety of levels in the social structure. The initial stability of the society was maintained by the imposition of the will of one group — the larger — on the other group — the smaller. A form of 'pillarisation' existed in which the larger, Protestant group was able to maintain a position of strength vis-à-vis the smaller, Roman Catholic group. Between them, these two 'pillars' propped up the society.

For approximately forty years after 1920, the social structure of Northern Ireland and the relationships between the two groups contained within that structure remained relatively static. This was a period of one-party rule at Stormont, exercised mainly by a Protestant landed and commercial upper class on behalf of themselves and their co-religionists. The main purpose of government was to keep the relationship between the two religious groups stable, with the Protestants in the dominant position. In this enterprise, the government was remarkably successful. In spite of periodic outbursts of violence, relations between the two groups *were* kept stable and turmoil on the scale of the post-1969 period was avoided. But in recent years the position has changed. As we have seen already, the start of that change may be located in the immediate post-World War Two years. One of the effects of these years was to produce the elements of a new Roman Catholic 'middle class' in Northern Ireland — a group of people who were highly educated and who had the aspirations and expectations normally associated with such educational status. These people, in turn, have been able to articulate the demands of the Roman Catholic minority, to provide the latter with a new type of leadership and to develop new focuses — like the Civil Rights campaign — to achieve their objectives.

This recent phenomenon appearing among the Roman Catholic minority is one of the new, dynamic forces that is changing the social structure of the society of Northern Ireland. As the social structure changes it is no longer possible to retain the static relationship between the two groups — a relationship on which the previous stability of the society so much depended. The maintenance of the boundaries between the two groups, boundaries which helped to give each a sense of security and identity, becomes more and more difficult to achieve as one group demands, and achieves, a greater degree of parity with the other, within the same society. The old position of dominant and subordinate groups is under attack and conflict, escalating into violence in some sections, ensues. During the conflict, the old pre-1969 political leaders in both groups are disappearing. The leadership of the Unionist party, the political expression of Protestantism, is taken away from the people who carried it for fifty years after the State was founded — the landed and commercial elite — while their last three representatives as Prime Ministers of Northern Ireland, O'Neill, Chichester-Clark and, before his death, Faulkner, were sent into political oblivion. At the same time, the old Nationalist and Republican leaders on the

Roman Catholic side have suffered the same fate. They are no longer relevant in the new social conflict that is emerging, and their place is taken by people in both religious groups who have a great deal in common with each other in terms of social background and education. Divisions and conflict remain *between* both groups but they also begin to appear *within* each group and it may be that the social context within which the people of Northern Ireland live is that of an emergent 'pluralist' society where the social and political issues characteristic of other pluralistic societies will eventually replace the breakdown across the religious divide.

Before that can happen, though, that religious divide has to be bridged, and it is this reality which makes any thought of a 'solution' to the Northern Ireland 'problem' unrealistic unless it is based on a lengthy time-span. As we have said before, the crucial group in this process are the Protestants of Northern Ireland. It has been demonstrated at some length earlier in this work how the religious beliefs of the Protestant majority are active in producing a world view which has direct consequences for the Northern Ireland Protestant's view of the nature of his State. It is, first and foremost, a *protective* State. It acts as a defence of Protestantism. There is a deep core of fear, suspicion, and hostility in Protestantism here against the Roman Catholic Church, particularly as it operates in the Republic of Ireland. This fear expresses itself on several closely linked levels. On the 'belief' level, the Ulster Protestant is convinced that his own particular form of Christianity will not be tolerated in a united Ireland and that the Roman Catholic Church will not rest until it has imposed *its* particular form throughout the entire geographical entity of Ireland. Whether this conviction is validly based is not the point; the fact is that it is very firmly established in Protestant minds. The latter cite the fate of the small Protestant minority in the Republic and the extent to which it has dwindled since 1920 as an indication of what will happen to them. On the 'political' level, Protestants in Northern Ireland fear that, given the Irish Roman Catholic Church's view of its relationship to the State and its 'rights' as an organisation to intervene in the political operations of that State, they would lose a great deal of the freedom and independence of judgment which is at the core of their conception of what it is to be a Christian. Again, they have cautionary examples to cite, including the Roman Catholic Church's quite open intervention in legislation affecting very personal concerns like divorce, contraception and even certain forms of welfare provision. In the face of all this there is a feeling that Protestant Christianity would come under severe threat in a united Ireland with not even the political mechanism of the State to appeal to for support.

As a result, Northern Ireland Protestants produced their own form of a link-up between religious belief and its political expression — a State which would guarantee the integrity they are seeking and provide a 'Protestant State for a Protestant people'. Such a political institution was maintained for a long time by a very close alliance between the Unionist party and the Orange Order, both solidly Protestant. It.provided the Protestant majority with a feeling of security through its political institution. They were able to adhere to the tenets of Protestantism, which insist on a separation of Church and State, so that no Church leader claimed the right to intervene in the State's affairs simply because he *was* a Church leader, while at the same time ensuring, through the Unionist party and the Orange Order, that only 'good Protestants' got into positions of power and political influence. In terms of the overall security of the State and its relationships with outside societies, they looked to Britain. I think it is helpful to look at the British 'link' in this light. Northern Ireland Protestants did not want, still do not want to become an integral part of the United Kingdom and do not regard themselves as 'British' in the sense of being content to be part of the political structure of the United Kingdom — as, say, Yorkshire or Kent — and ruled directly from Westminster.[1] Britain's role is that of 'protector' of the State, not its ruler. David Miller's arguments along these lines are persuasive and seen to match the contemporary situation.[2] Northern Ireland's Protestants seem to regard their relationship with Britain as 'contractual' i.e. both States are seen as partners to a 'contract' by which Britain is obliged to provide support and assistance to

Northern Ireland in return for services rendered in the past and likely to be rendered in the future. In this sense, Britain acts as 'guarantor' for the maintenance of the Northern Ireland State and provides the society of Northern Ireland with the ultimate line of defence.

The survey data indicate that many Roman Catholics, the minority in Northern Ireland, want also to be a part of that society. They wish to share in it with their Protestant fellow citizens and take their rightful place in running its affairs. Just as the evidence indicates that most Protestants do not want to be an integral part of Britain, so it also shows that most Roman Catholics do not want to be part of a united Ireland. The latter see their future in a Northern Ireland society where they can fulfil their aspirations and develop a rewarding life-style. Why, then, cannot there be peace and harmony? In attempting part of an answer to that question it is necessary to recall our earlier statement that the Northern Ireland State is regarded by the majority as a *Protestant* State set up to preserve the integrity of *Protestantism*. That integrity can be attacked in many ways of which physical violence is only one. It can be attacked by allowing, for example, Roman Catholics to increase their level of influence and affluence and therefore beginning to allow them into positions where they can start to influence the future destiny of the society. This is precisely what happened in the start of the present 'troubles' in the 1960s. It was not the activities of the IRA which provoked the violent conflict of the late 1960s. Their campaign had petered out in failure in 1962 and had made very little impact in the years during which it had been officially waged. The starting point for the conflict was a peaceful campaign for the extension of civil rights to all members of Northern Ireland's society. This was regarded with deep concern by a section of the Protestant population, especially that section represented by the Rev. Ian Paisley, who viewed any change of the status quo as representing a threat to the integrity of their society and the beginnings of a move to force them into a united Ireland. This concern spread when the then Prime Minister, O'Neill, made some concessions to the demands of the campaigners — a move which was later to cost him his position. It appeared as if Protestant Northern Ireland really was under attack; 'Civil Rights', which was benefiting Roman Catholics, was identified as 'Republicanism' which was also associated with Roman Catholics, and this identification brought about a violent reaction among Protestants. In this way, a movement for social reform which was developing out of social change became quickly regarded as an attack on the very structure of the society itself and the State which was its political expression. Physical violence was used against some sections of the minority population and this brought back the IRA, first in a defensive role and later in an offensive one, backed by the old ideology.

The events which have followed are too well known to need recounting. Activities by groups on both sides of the religious divide have helped to convince some Protestants that they were right in their interpretation of the activities of the mid 1960s, and some Roman Catholics that they will not receive fair and just treatment in Northern Ireland's society. The intervention of the British Army, in response to Britain's 'contractual' obligation to Northern Ireland, as a force designed to prevent sections of both groups from destroying each other, has produced its own dynamic. This intervention has been interpreted by some amongst the Roman Catholics as yet another expression of British 'imperialism' and has helped to fan the smouldering embers of the dying fire of Republicanism among, now, a restricted section of the minority group. This revival of Republicanism, coupled with the support it is given by Roman Catholic clergy, who condemn the activities of the IRA but bury its 'heroes' with the full pomp and panoply of the Roman Catholic Church and therefore legitimate their actions, fuels Protestant fears and reinforces their suspicions of the intentions of their Roman Catholic fellow-citizens.

This is one of the complex reasons contributing to the length of the present outbreak. All attempts at negotiation and compromise have foundered on the rock of the Protestant fear of being absorbed into the Republic of Ireland and lack of trust in any assurances that this will not happen. Protestant leaders who have attempted negotiation and compromise have rapidly found themselves without an effective following. This was finally and conclusively demonstrated by the failure of the power-sharing experiment of 1974, under pressure from the Ulster Workers' Council and the Reverend Ian Paisley, and the consequent ending of the political career of the last Unionist Prime Minister of Northern Ireland — Brian Faulkner. On the basis of the available evidence one can say that the peace and harmony, mentioned earlier, will not come to Northern Ireland until Protestants here cease to regard Roman Catholics as agents of the Irish Republic and as representatives of a Church that will not respect their integrity as fellow Christians. Only when this happens will the Protestants consent to share their society on equal terms with the Catholics. This society will be one that cannot return to the static state of its first forty years of existence — a fact which many Protestants are aware of and which makes them feel that they are fighting a desperate rearguard action to preserve their integrity — but it will be a society open to the 'modernising' forces already operating upon it. During the process the religious institution may also evolve to the point that it may become apparent that religious beliefs do not have to be expressed in organisations dominated by a 'fortress' mentality but can find other forms of social expression without losing their integrity as beliefs. Religious beliefs do not have to disappear but in their social form they may have to evolve; and in this evolution they may avoid destructive polarisation and not only assist in keeping the society of Northern Ireland intact but help it to become peaceful and prosperous.

Appendix:

Study of a Community in Northern Ireland

There have been a number of surveys of Protestants and Roman Catholics in Northern Ireland; reference has been made to them in the text and in the Bibliography. What follows here should be regarded as a 'case study' demonstrating some of the characteristics and attitudes of a sample of the people — Protestants and Roman Catholics — who make up the population of a small town in the northern part of the province. It has been included here not only because it contains original, primary data but also because it demonstrates that even in a small, rural community where there is an apparently high degree of mutual acceptance and sympathy between Protestants and Roman Catholics, there is still a 'hard core' of people of both religions who will not accept the other. This 'non-acceptance' sometimes amounts to positive hostility and acts of violence, the latest of which, on 11 October 1981, was the virtual destruction of the new Roman Catholic church in the town by a bomb planted by Protestant extremists.

The work here reported on is part of a larger piece of research, funded by the Ford Foundation through its Committee on Social Research in Ireland.

The study was conducted in 1977 through the use of an interview schedule containing questions relating to religion, national identity, education and social class. Out of a total population of 4,999 a random sample of 450 adults was selected from the electoral rolls and 297 interviews completed. Of the respondents, 183 were Protestants and 106 were Catholics, with the remainder being of another or no religion.

The purpose of this extract is obviously not to survey and analyse the whole range of data available from the study but to concentrate on certain specific points. First of all it seemed important to establish at the outset the actual level of religious practice — or stated religious practice — which obtained amongst the people of the town in question.

Secondly, questions were asked relating to the way in which the respondents saw themselves in terms of 'national identity'. What was being investigated here was the extent to which people regarded themselves as an integral part of a society with a strong sense of nationalism and a distinct cultural tradition. Where did people feel that they 'belonged'; with whom did they automatically identify when asked the question 'what do you see yourself as?' Allied to this, and emphasising the political dimension of this identification, was the question of the type of government which most respondents would prefer. A whole range of alternative forms of government were placed before the respondents and their answers are reported on below.

There is also the question of the degree of attachment the people of the town felt for their own region and for Northern Ireland as a whole. The question may be posed that, as there is so much conflict and unhappiness in Northern Ireland, why is not emigration greatly intensified? The answer to that could be that many more people would in fact leave if there were ample opportunities near at hand — in mainland Britain for instance — for employment, but that unemployment is a serious problem in the United Kingdom generally and it is not a propitious time to move. The problem with this answer is that it infers that people do really want to move and only current economic circumstances are keeping them where they are. This may well be true; but it may also be the case that one of the reasons for the present disturbances is that people are attached to their part of their homeland and consider it well worth fighting over.

Finally, some of the data collected concerning the attitudes of Protestant and Catholics in the town towards each other is reported on here. Material has been selected relating to questions asked about attitudes towards neighbours, working relationships with people of the opposite religion, intermarriage and integrated schooling. What follows, then, is first a discussion of religious practice, to establish some basic appreciation of the strength of both Protestantism and Roman Catholicism in this respect and in comparison with the rest of the UK, national and local identification, and attitudes between Protestants and Catholics on a number of issues. In the tables which follow, the sample population has been divided on religious grounds and the answers categorised according to membership of the Protestant or Catholic faiths.

Table 1
How often do you go to church for services or prayer?

	Protestants %	Catholics %	other %	all %
Daily	1.3	6.0	0.0	3.0
More than once a week	5.3	19.0	43.0	10.4
Weekly	30.4	59.0	14.0	40.2
At least monthly	28.3	4.0	0.0	18.5
Occasionally/hardly ever	31.7	7.0	0.0	21.5
Never	2.4	6.0	43.0	6.1
Not applicable	0.6	0.0	0.0	0.3

Total 100.0%
Number 297

Table 2

Which form of government in Northern Ireland would you most prefer?

	Protestants %	Catholics %	other %	all %
Continuation of direct rule from Westminster	16.0	14.0	42.5	15.9
A totally independent Northern Ireland government	2.2	2.0	0.0	2.4
Complete integration with Britain	20.5	5.0	0.0	14.1
Integration into a united Ireland	0.6	14.0	0.0	5.4
Return to the system before the present trouble started	23.8	15.0	15.0	20.5
A government from Stormont in which the two communities share power	33.8	50.0	28.5	39.4
Other	0.6	0.0	0.0	0.3
Don't know	1.7	0.0	0.0	1.0
No answer	0.8	0.0	14.0	1.0

Total 100.0%
Number 297

Table 3
How do you usually think of yourself?

	Protestants %	Catholics %	other %	all %
British	60.9	32.0	86.0	51.2
Irish	7.4	54.0	0.0	23.6
Ulster	21.6	3.0	0.0	14.5
Sometimes British/ sometimes Irish	4.9	4.0	0.0	4.4
Anglo-Irish	0.5	2.0	0.0	1.0
Northern Irish	0.0	1.0	0.0	0.3
Don't know	0.7	0.0	0.0	0.3
Other	1.2	4.0	14.0	2.7
No answer	2.8	1.0	0.0	2.0
			Total	100.0%
			Number	297

Table 4
Have you ever seriously considered emigrating from Northern Ireland?

	Protestants %	Catholics %	other %	all %
Yes	18.2	23.5	0.0	19.9
No	80.6	75.5	100.0	78.8
No answer	1.2	1.0	0.0	1.3
			Total	100.0%
			Number	297

Table 5
I would be quite happy if someone of the other religion moved in next
door tomorrow

	Protestants %	Catholics %	other %	all %
Agree strongly	81.7	89.0	71.5	83.8
Agree a little	13.9	10.0	28.5	12.8
Disagree a little	2.5	1.0	0.0	2.4
Disagree strongly	1.3	0.0	0.0	0.7
Don't know	0.6	0.0	0.0	0.3
			Total	100.0%
			Number	297

Table 6
I would be quite happy to have someone of the other religion as my
boss

	Protestants %	Catholics %	other %	all %
Agree strongly	74.9	85.0	72.0	78.5
Agree a little	14.8	13.0	14.0	14.1
Disagree a little	5.9	1.0	0.0	4.0
Disagree strongly	3.3	1.0	14.0	2.7
Don't know	1.1	0.0	0.0	0.7
			Total	100.0%
			Number	297

Table 7

What proportion of your relatives by marriage are (Roman Catholic/Protestant) of the other religion?

	Protestants %	Catholics %	other %	all %
All	1.7	2.0	0.0	1.7
Most	1.2	3.0	0.0	1.7
Half	3.3	12.0	0.0	6.4
Less than half	29.2	48.0	14.5	36.0
None	61.2	32.0	56.5	50.5
Don't know	3.4	3.0	29.0	3.7
			Total	100.0%
			Number	297

Table 8

If a person of the same religion as yourself decided to marry a Roman Catholic/Protestant would you . . .

	Protestants %	Catholics %	other %	all %
Disapprove strongly	14.3	2.5	57.0	11.8
Disapprove somewhat	12.9	8.5	0.0	10.8
Have no feelings one way or the other	18.4	25.5	0.0	20.5
Approve somewhat	1.7	6.0	0.0	3.1
Approve strongly	2.0	4.0	0.0	2.7
Feel it depends on the individual	48.9	52.5	43.0	49.8
Don't know	1.8	1.0	0.0	1.3
			Total	100.0%
			Number	297

Table 9

If a member of your family decided to marry a Roman Catholic/
Protestant would you . . .

	Protestants %	Catholics %	other %	all %
Disapprove strongly	26.0	8.8	57.0	20.9
Disapprove somewhat	21.3	13.8	0.0	17.8
Have no feeling one way or the other	13.9	21.8	0.0	16.5
Approve somewhat	0.7	6.9	0.0	2.7
Approve strongly	1.0	2.9	0.0	1.7
Feel it depends on the individual	36.0	44.9	43.0	39.4
Don't know	1.1	0.9	0.0	1.0
			Total Number	100.0% 297

Table 10

The existence of separate Protestant and Roman Catholic neighbourhoods is one of the causes of the troubles

	Protestants %	Catholics %	other %	all %
Agree strongly	53.7	52.0	43.0	54.2
Agree a little	26.6	22.5	0.0	24.9
Disagree a little	12.0	8.5	43.0	11.4
Disagree strongly	7.3	9.5	14.0	8.8
Don't know	0.4	7.5	0.0	0.7
			Total Number	100.0% 297

Table 11
It is sometimes said that in parts of Northern Ireland Catholics are treated unfairly. Do you think this is true, or not?

	Protestants %	Catholics %	other %	all %
Yes; treated unfairly	23.6	58.0	14.6	36.0
No	65.2	24.0	56.4	50.2
Don't know	11.2	18.0	29.0	13.8
			Total	100.0%
			Number	297

Table 12
It is sometimes said that in parts of Northern Ireland Protestants are treated unfairly. Do you think this is true, or not?

	Protestants %	Catholics %	other %	all %
Yes; treated unfairly	35.6	36.0	29.0	35.7
No	51.9	41.0	43.0	47.8
Don't know	12.5	23.0	28.0	16.5
			Total	100.0%
			Number	297

Table 13
Do you think that *in principle* unifying the Protestant and Catholic Churches is . . .

	Protestants %	Catholics %	other %	all %
Desirable	29.6	53.0	28.7	38.0
Undesirable	34.6	10.0	28.7	25.9
Depends	27.1	30.0	28.7	27.9
Don't know	8.3	6.0	13.9	7.5
No answer	0.4	1.0	0.0	0.7

Total 100.0%
Number 297

Table 14
Do you think that *in practice* unifying the Churches is . . .

	Protestants %	Catholics %	other %	all %
Possible	11.4	28.0	14.0	17.5
Impossible	63.0	29.0	86.0	51.5
Depends	22.0	34.0	0.0	25.6
Don't know	3.2	8.0	0.0	4.7
No answer	0.4	1.0	0.0	0.7

Total 100.0%
Number 297

The data presented have only been analysed on the basis of a Protestant-Catholic categorisation. The influence of major variables like the age, sex and occupation of the respondents has not yet been examined. Further analysis involving these variables is obviously of importance but it would seem that certain tentative conclusions may be drawn from the data already reported.

There is an obviously wide area of agreement between the two religious groups on the questions of neighbourhood, work and friendship. From the responses to the questions in these areas a picture emerges of a large proportion of Protestants and Catholics willing to live and work together and to share friendships across the religious divide. There is no evidence here of ghettoisation in its widest sense. To be effective, ghettoisation must involve not only segregated living areas but also a feeling of alienation between groups over a wide range of social relationships, particularly those involving neighbourliness and close friendships. The data indicate that most people in the town live in mixed religious neighbourhoods and engage in close inter-religious relationships. This is not to say that each group does not have some sense of difference from the other – this point will be referred to again later – but the sense of distinctiveness is not sufficiently strong or widespread to prevent social intercourse across the religious divide.

This is in contrast to what is known of the situation in Belfast and Derry where Protestants and Catholics of the working and lower-middle-class groups *do* live in isolation from each other, both physically and socially. It may be that, sociologically, the reason for this contrast is bound up with the size and visibility of the groups in question. The place surveyed is a small country town, with not much scope for the development of two separate and hostile communities. Belfast, on the other hand, is a large city by the standards of the United Kingdom and both groups have had the opportunity, in terms of population and financial resources, to develop actual and symbolic manifestations of their separateness. The physical size and resources of the 'Catholic' area of Belfast are sufficient to allow most of its inhabitants to live out their daily lives with only relatively infrequent excursions into other areas of the city. Similarly, Catholics in the city have at their disposal an entire and separate education system, including two Colleges of Education to provide teachers for that system. To the Protestants of Belfast, then, Catholics appear not only to be different but to be emphasising that difference. They – the Catholics – are also sufficiently large in numbers to constitute a 'threat' to their

immediate neighbours, and this is a major factor in promoting the level of violence in the city. The same factors
are at work in Derry, with the added feature of that city's
particular historical tradition. Derry has a special place in
both Protestant and Catholic mythology in that its successful resistance to the (Catholic) forces of James II is regarded
as the turning point in securing the province for the Protestants. This gives Derry a central, symbolic significance
which heightens the tensions between Protestants and
Catholics in the city and makes it unrepresentative of the
province as a whole.

The responses to the question of the government of the
province indicate an unexpected consensus between the two
religious groups. It has been assumed by the historical and
political commentators on conditions in Ulster that one of
the chief factors promoting the internal division — and hence
disruption — of the society was the rejection on the part of
the Catholics of any form of government which did not
establish the province firmly within the Republic of Ireland.

The data go a long way to deny this view. There is division
about the *form* of government the society should have,
particularly among the Protestants, but almost no division
at all on the question of whether such a government should
exist. The large majority of Catholics in the sample reject
integration either into a united Ireland or into the United
Kingdom. By far the biggest proportion of Catholics want a
form of power-sharing with the Protestants, a situation which
would validate their position as full and equal members of
the same society. The Protestants are equally firm in their
rejection of integration into a larger unit but are much more
divided than the Catholics on the form their own government
should take. A substantial proportion of them, but not a
majority, would accept power-sharing, but there is no real
consensus among them.

On the question of mixed marriages there is again no
evidence of a rigid divide between the two groups. The Protestants are almost equally split between those who would
and those who would not accept, in theory, marriages
across the religious divide. In practice, a substantial minority
of Protestants *do* have relatives by marriage from the other

religion. The Catholics seem to be more accepting of the idea of mixed marriages and a larger proportion of them than Protestants have relatives by marriage from the other religion. The discrepancy between the two groups may be the result of the assumption on the part of both Catholics and Protestants that a mixed marriage means that in religion the Catholic partner will be the dominant one. Whatever the reasons for the differences in attitude and practice between the two groups, the fact remains that there is no evidence of an inflexible endogamy existing here, and previous assumptions of the rarity of inter-religious marriage need to be revised.

In terms of mutual 'sympathy' between the two groups, the evidence does indicate some differences between Protestants and Catholics. The data collected on the responses to the statements that each religious group has been treated unfairly, that Protestants and Catholics are 'alike' and that both groups think and feel the same about most things, show the Catholics responding more 'positively' than the Protestants in all these areas. This may be because Catholics are more 'tender-minded' than the Protestants, but it may also result from a feeling on the part of the Catholics that they have more to gain by blending with Protestants than vice versa. The evidence from the question on government indicated that Catholics are seeking equal partnership within the province and it would be reasonable to suppose that they would want to emphasise the likenesses between themselves and the other religious group.

In general, then, the data indicate that there are divisions *between* Protestants and Catholics but there are also divisions within each group. Among some members of both groups there is a sense of 'separateness' from members of the other religion. There is a hard core of people within the Protestants who wish to retain the boundaries between them and the Catholics; the evidence from a number of items shows this. The same is true, to a lesser extent, among the Catholic group. But there is also a great deal of evidence to indicate that among large proportions of both groups strict boundaries in a large area of social relationships are not being maintained, either in theory or in practice. This may signal the emergence of areas of common ground between the two groups. It may also be instrumental in triggering off violent conflict as the 'separatists' of both groups see their previous positions threatened by the increasing 'nearness' of the other. For the Protestants, the erosion of boundaries between themselves and Roman Catholics may be seen as threatening their defensive dominance and putting the stability of the State in question. For those Roman Catholics who are dedicated to the ideas of Republicanism, close relationships with Protestants may imply working together as fellow-citizens and hence accepting the validity of the Northern Ireland State. In this context, social conditions that encourage mixing across the religious divide may also be significant in provoking violence and hostility amongst those groups on both sides who wish to emphasise their irreconcilable differences.

Notes

Introduction
(pp. 1—4)

1. For a good account of the foundation and development of the Northern Ireland Labour Party see M. Farrell, *Northern Ireland: The Orange State* (London: Pluto Press 1976).
2. The book produced by the *Sunday Times* Insight Team, *Ulster* (Penguin 1972) contains a well-researched analysis of this campaign.
3. This point is returned to in Chapter 6.

Chapter 1
Overview (pp. 5—28)

1. See, for instance, J. C. Beckett, *The Making of Modern Ireland* (Faber 1966); F. S. L. Lyons, *Ireland since the Famine* (Fontana 1973); and the Gill History of Ireland series (Gill and Macmillan 1972-75).
2. How 'temporarily' this was may be demonstrated by the Civil War of 1922-23 and the continuing problem with the Irish Republican Army, in various forms. The fact that the IRA still operates in the Republic and regards the Dublin government, of whatever political colour, as one of its prime opponents is not, I think, sufficiently appreciated by observers of the Northern Ireland scene.
3. There is a very readable account of some aspects of this period in George Dangerfield's *The Strange Death of Liberal England* (Macgibbon and Kee 1966).
4. For a full account of this period in Northern Ireland see A. T. Q. Stewart, *The Ulster Crisis* (Faber 1967).
5. A. T. Q. Stewart, op. cit.
6. Transcription from *The Times*, 20 September 1912, quoted in A. C. Hepburn, *The Conflict of Nationality in Modern Ireland* (Edward Arnold 1980), p. 76.
7. See A. T. Q. Stewart, op. cit.
8. The details of this violent conflict are referred to throughout this text.
9. HMSO *Census of Population*, Belfast 1971. The figures regarding

Protestant/Roman Catholic affiliation in this report are inexact, to a certain degree, as approximately 9 per cent of the total population of Northern Ireland refused to state their religion on the 1971 census form. It is worth while mentioning here that Northern Ireland is the only part of the United Kingdom where residents are required to state their religion on the census form. In the remainder of the UK such a question would be regarded as unethical — an unwarrantable intrusion on the privacy of the individual.

10. See D. P. Barrit and C. F. Carter, *The Northern Ireland Problem* (Oxford University Press, revised edn 1972), p. 19. The analysis which this book presents has, in some respects, been rendered out of date by more recent work but it still constitutes perhaps the best short introduction to the study of contemporary Northern Ireland.

11. See 1971 census, op. cit.

12. The work of R. Deutsch and V. Magowan in *Northern Ireland, Chronology of Events* (Belfast: Blackstaff), vol. 1: *1968-71* (1973). vol. 2: *1971-73* (1974) provides some of the data on which these statements are based. My own study of a country town where the religious breakdown of the population almost exactly replicates that of Northern Ireland generally, also supports the analysis. See Appendix.

13. In this connection see the following discussion of the development of religious group relations in Belfast.

14. This experience now (1981) adds up to seven years, during which I have been both 'observer' and 'participant' in the society of Northern Ireland.

15. It has provided several 'Orange' battle-cries, of which 'No Surrender' is probably the best known.

16. For most of this and the ensuing paragraphs on Belfast I have drawn heavily on the collection of essays edited by J. C. Beckett and R. Glasscock, *Belfast: Origin and Growth of an Industrial City* (BBC Publications 1967). The analysis of 'ghettoisation' is, however, my own and I must accept full responsibility for it. The evidence produced in Beckett and Glasscock is largely historical. In terms of 'ghettoisation' it has been supplemented by recent studies of Belfast, in particular those of F. W. Boal, R. C. Murray and M. A. Poole as summarised in their 'Belfast: the Urban Encapsulation of a National Conflict' in S. E. Clarke and L. Obler (eds.), *Urban Ethnic Conflict A Comparative Perspective* (University of North Carolina 1976).

Evidence for ghettoisation in Derry may be found in F. Boal, and A. Robinson, 'Close Together and Far Apart', *Community Forum*, vol. 2, no. 3, 1972.

17. See Chapters 3, 4 and 5.

18. In this connection see the study by Frank Burton of one of the Roman Catholic areas of Belfast, *The Politics of Legitimacy: Struggles in a Belfast Community* (Routledge and Kegan Paul 1978).

19. Burton, op. cit.
20. Quoted by J. C. Beckett, in Beckett and Glasscock, op. cit.
21. J. C. Beckett, in Beckett and Glasscock, op. cit.
22. A. C. Hepburn, ed., *Minorities in History* (Edward Arnold 1978), p. 84, quoting the Royal Commission of Inquiry into the Belfast Riots (British Parliamentary Papers 1857-8, xxxvi), p. 241.
23. See, for instance, my study of Irish immigrants in Britain, *Urban Catholics* (Geoffrey Chapman 1967).
24. E. Jones, 'Late Victorian Belfast: 1850-1900' in Beckett and Glasscock, op. cit.
25. See Darby, op. cit.
26. For a detailed account of this movement see P. Arthur, *The People's Democracy* (Blackstaff 1973).

Chapter 2
Explanations of the Northern Ireland Problem (pp. 29—56)
1. There has been an abundance of literature that has adopted this approach. Two good examples are the *Handbook of the Ulster Question* (North Eastern Boundary Bureau 1923) and F. Gallagher, *The Indivisible Island: The Story of the Partition of Ireland* (Gollancz 1957).
2. Again, there is an abundance of literature which demonstrates this approach and which may be found summarised in Darby's Bibliography (1976). To appreciate, however, how *alive* this political interpretation is, it is necessary to read the relevant newspapers which reflect this point of view. Probably the most 'extreme' of these journals is the *Republican News*, published in Dublin and Belfast.
   For a Protestant view of Republicanism see *Republicanism, The Aims, Ideals and Methods of Irish Republicanism* (Report of the Committee on National and International Problems to the General Assembly of the Presbyterian Church in Ireland 1974).
3. *Republican News*, op. cit.
4. D. Hyde, *The Revival of Irish Literature and Other Addresses* (T. Fisher Unwin 1894), pp. 126-7, quoted in A. C. Hepburn, *Conflict of Nationality in Modern Ireland* (Edward Arnold 1980), p. 62.
5. D. P. Moran, 'The Pale and the Gael' in *The Philosophy of Irish Ireland* (Dublin: James Duffy 1905), pp. 37-47, quoted in Hepburn, op. cit., p. 63.
6. See for example, the work of Emmet Larkin, listed in the Bibliography, in particular his article on 'The Devotional Revolution in Ireland, 1850-1875' *A. H. R. (American Historical Review)*, vol. lxxvii, 3 June 1972.
7. *The Leader*, 27 July 1901, quoted in Hepburn, op. cit., p. 65.
8. See J. Whyte, 'Interpretations of the Northern Ireland Problem: an Appraisal' *Economic and Social Review*, vol. ix, no. 4, July 1978; also Darby, op. cit.

9. See, for example, the evidence from my study (Appendix) relating to choice of government; and the work of Richard Rose, op. cit.

10. See Farrell, op. cit; and Bew, Gibbon and Patterson *The State in Northern Ireland, 1921-72* (Manchester University Press 1979).

11. Note also, in this extract, the implicit equation of 'religion' with 'ideology' in the last three lines. It is, I think, important in the sociological sense to distinguish between religion and ideology; the former may constitute the basis of the latter as part of a 'world view' but should not be regarded as identical with it, otherwise 'Protestantism' and 'Roman Catholicism' as belief systems occupy the same category as 'Conservatism', 'Fascism', 'Communism' and 'Socialism'. That they do *not* fit into this category is demonstrated by the fact that these ideologies, contrary to each other as they are, draw adherents from both Protestantism and Roman Catholicism.

Chapter 3
The Effect of Religious Belief on the Conflict in Northern Ireland
(pp. 57—88)

1. See Bibliography.

2. Wells and Mawhinney have in fact pointed to the differences in outlook and beliefs among Protestants and Roman Catholics in Northern Ireland and have hinted at the connections these may have with conflicting views of the relationship between 'Church' and 'State'. See R. A. Wells and B. S. Mawhinney, *Conflict and Christianity in Northern Ireland*, (Michigan: Erdmans 1975).

3. Max Weber, 'The Social Psychology of the World Religions' in H. Gerth and C. W. Mills, eds., *From Max Weber* (New York: OUP 1968 edn).

4. R. Mehl, *The Sociology of Protestantism* (SCM 1970), p. xii.

5. Darby has adequately summarised this period. See Darby, op. cit.

6. For a full account of this organisation see T. Gray, *The Orange Order* (Bodley Head 1972).

7. See Rose, op. cit. and J. F. Harbinson, *The Ulster Unionist Party* (Blackstaff 1973).

8. J. Darby, op. cit., p. 169.

9. See, for example, the *Sunday Times* leader already quoted and O'Farrell's comments referred to later in this chapter.

10. Quoted in F. Wright, 'Protestant Ideology and Politics in Ulster', *European Journal of Sociology*, vol. xiv, no. 2, 1973.

11. See also the general statements on Protestantism made by Mehl, op. cit., p. 158.

12. This is the argument which seems to form the underlying bases of a number of analyses currently put forward by sociologists of religion. See, for example, T. Luckmann, *The Invisible Religion* (Macmillan 1967) and B. Wilson, *Contemporary Transformations of Religion* (Clarendon Press 1979). This and other arguments will be referred to later in this work.

13. See Chapters 5 and 6.
14. For the following paragraphs I have drawn to some extent upon the insights developed by Weber and Parsons: see M. Weber, *The Sociology of Religion* (Methuen 1965) and T. Parsons, *Action Theory and the Human Condition* (New York: Free Press 1978), Chapter 9.
15. See Larkin, op. cit.
16. This position has changed since 1978.
17. The most quoted example of such intervention occurred in the early 1950s when the Roman Catholic hierarchy effectively prevented the passing of legislation aimed at improving family welfare. For a detached account of this episode see J. H. Whyte, *Church and State in Modern Ireland, 1923-1970* (Gill and Macmillan 1971).

Chapter 4
'Modernisation' and Northern Ireland (pp. 89—105)
1. See the evidence produced by my study (Appendix) and the work of Richard Rose, op. cit.
2. For a sensitive and illuminating discussion of 'cultures' within Ireland from this standpoint see F. S. L. Lyons, *Culture and Anarchy in Ireland 1890-1939* (Clarendon Press 1979).
3. See the *Report* produced by the Committee on Irish Language Attitudes Research. This report is cyclostyled and its flyleaf indicates that it is a *Report as submitted to the Minister of the Gaeltacht*, October 1975.
4. See, for instance, the work of E. Gellner, *Thought and Change* (Weidenfeld and Nicolson 1964).
5. For corroborative evidence of this see, for example, K. Boyle, T. Hadden and P. Hillyard in *Ten Years After* and Bew *et. al.* (1979), op. cit., p. 167. The latter in commenting on the statistics make the point that for the Roman Catholic population *as a whole* there has not been a marked increase in affluence and that there are some indications of downward social mobility among Roman Catholics. They do, however, admit to the fact that 'The proportion of Catholics in professional and managerial occupations has risen sharply — more sharply in fact than the population of the province as a whole.' The exact proportions of Protestant and Roman Catholic university students is not now ascertainable through official statistics. There are, no doubt, good political reasons for this. My own impressions of the over-representation of Roman Catholic students in the university population is supported by the fact that my own university is sometimes referred to as 'Vatican City' by the local inhabitants of the area. Also, I attempted in 1977 to investigate the friendship patterns between Protestant and Roman Catholic students at NUU to see if there was substantial mixing across the religious divide. One of my questionnaires

was returned blank, with the anguished question, 'Are there any students of the Protestant faith in this university?' written across it in block capitals.

Chapter 5
Is Religion Declining in Importance? (pp. 106–117)

1. How difficult should be apparent from the preceding argument of this work and from the continuing violent conflict in Northern Ireland. One analyst who has, in my view, put the correct emphasis on the facts that religious beliefs live and are very influential in affecting the present situation in Northern Ireland is Richard Rose. See Rose, op. cit., especially pp. 401 and following.
2. See, for example, Luckmann (1967), and Caporale and Grumelli (1971).
3. See, for example, Berger (1969).
4. Cf. R. Bellah in Caporale and Grumelli (1971).
5. For a comprehensive discussion of the view that the importance of religion is declining in Western society and that an 'inevitable' process of 'secularisation' is taking place, see Martin (1978). Martin powerfully argues against the simplicity of this view.
6. Luckmann, op. cit., 1971.
7. David Martin has provided a very useful summary of the statistics which add to this picture of organised religion in England. See Martin (1967).
8. See Darby *et. al.* (1977).

Chapter 6
Towards a Sociological Analysis of Northern Ireland Society (pp. 118–126)

1. See the evidence in the Appendix and the results produced by Rose's much more comprehensive survey.
2. See Miller (1978).

Select Bibliography

This bibliography is not intended as a comprehensive list of the work published on Northern Ireland; the best bibliographies in this respect may be found in J. Darby (1976) and J. Whyte (1978) and the reader is recommended to them. For the researcher interested in delving deeply into the subject of Northern Ireland the work of Darby and Whyte may be supplemented by consulting the *Registers* of research completed or in progress. Of these, two may be mentioned — the *Register* (1981) recently completed by J. Darby, N. Dodge and A. C. Hepburn of the Centre for the Study of Conflict, New University of Ulster, Coleraine, Northern Ireland and the *Register* produced by the Centre for Policy Studies at Strathclyde University, Glasgow. Newspapers and pamphlets referred to in the text are not listed in the Bibliography but full details relating to them may be found in the Notes.

Acquaviva, S. S., *The Decline of the Sacred in Industrial Society*, Oxford: Blackwell 1979 edn.

Arthur, P.; *The People's Democracy, 1967-73*, Belfast: Blackstaff 1974

Barritt, D. P. and C. F. Carter, *The Northern Ireland Problem: A Study in Group Relations*, London: OUP 2nd edn. 1972

Beckett, J. C., *The Making of Modern Ireland, 1603-1923*, London: Faber and Faber 1978 edn.

Beckett, J. C. and R. E. Glasscock, eds., *Belfast: Origin and Growth of an Industrial City*, London: BBC 1967

Bellah, R. N., *Beyond Belief*, New York: Harper and Row 1970

Berger, P. L., *A Rumour of Angels*, Allen Lane, The Penguin Press 1970

Berger, P. L., *The Social Reality of Religion*, London: Faber and Faber 1969

Bew, P., P. Gibbon and H. Patterson, *The State in Northern Ireland, 1921-72*, Manchester UP 1979

Birrell, D., 'Relative Deprivation as a Factor in Conflict in Northern Ireland', *Sociological Review*, vol. 20, no. 3, pp. 317-47

Blaxter, L. et. al., *Irish Rural Society: A Selected Bibliography 1920-1972*, 1972, unpublished

Boal, F. W., R. C. Murray and M. A. Poole, 'Belfast: the Urban Encapsulation of a National Conflict' in S. E. Clarke and L. Obler, eds., *Urban Ethnic Conflict: A Comparative Perspective*, University of North Carolina 1976

Boal, F. and A. Robinson, 'Close Together and Far Apart', *Community Forum*, vol. 2, no. 3, 1972

Borhek, J. T. and R. F. Curtis, *A Sociology of Belief*, New York 1975

Bossy, J., *The English Catholic Community*, London: Darton, Longman and Todd 1975

Budd, S., *Sociologists and Religion*, London: Collier Macmillan 1973

Budge, I. and C. O'Leary, *Belfast: Approach to Crisis – A Study of Belfast Politics, 1613-1970*, London: Macmillan 1973

Burton, F., *The Politics of Legitimacy: Struggles in a Belfast Community*, London: Routledge and Kegan Paul 1978

Caporale, R. and A. Grumelli, eds., *The Culture of Unbelief*, Berkeley: University of California Press 1971

Carson, A. R. H., *Bibliography of the City and County of Londonderry*, New University of Ulster: ref. ZDA990L.8

Coman, P., *Catholics and the Welfare State*, London: Longman 1977

Dangerfield, G., *The Strange Death of Liberal England*, London: MacGibbon and Kee, 1966 edn.

Darby, J., *Conflict in Northern Ireland*, Dublin: Gill and Macmillan 1976

De Paor, L., *Divided Ulster*, Harmondsworth, Mdx: Penguin 1971

Deutsch, R. and V. Magowan, *Northern Ireland, Chronology of Events*, vol. 1, 1973, vol. 2, 1974, Belfast: Blackstaff

Dillon, M. and D. Lehane, *Political Murder in Northern Ireland*, Harmondsworth, Mdx: Penguin 1973

Disturbances in Northern Ireland, Report of the Commission appointed by the Governor of Northern Ireland, Belfast: HMSO 1969 Cmd 532

Durkheim, E., *The Elementary Forms of Religious Life*, New York: Free Press, 1954

Easthope, G., 'Religious War in Northern Ireland', *Sociology*, Sept. 1976

Edwards, L. P., *The Natural History of Revolution*, Chicago: University of Chicago Press 1970 edn.

Edwards, O. D., *The Sins of Our Fathers*, Dublin: Gill and Macmillan 1970

Elliott, R. and J. Hickie, *Ulster*, London: Longman 1971

Epstein, A. L., *Ethos and Identity*, London: Tavistock 1978

Evans, E. Estyn, *The Personality of Ireland*, Cambridge University Press 1973

Evason, E., 'Northern Ireland's Peace Movement', *Community Development Journal*, vol. 12, no. 2, April 1977

Farrell, M., *Northern Ireland: The Orange State*, London: Pluto Press 1976

Gallagher, F., *The Indivisible Island: The Story of the Partition of Ireland*, London: Gollancz 1957

Gellner, E., *Thought and Change*, London: Weidenfeld and Nicolson 1964

Gerth, H. and C. W. Mills, eds. *From Max Weber*, New York: OUP 1968

Gibbon, P., 'The Dialectic of Religion and Class in Ulster', *New Left Review*, 55, May-June 1969

Glock, C. and R. Stark, *Religion and Society in Tension*, New York: Rand McNally 1973

Golde, G., *Catholics and Protestants*, New York: Academic Press 1975

Gray, T., *The Orange Order*, London: The Bodley Head 1972

Greeley, A. M., *The Denominational Society*, Illinois: Scott Foresman 1972

Greeley, A. M., *Religion in the Year 2000*, New York: Sheed and Ward 1969

Greeley, A. M., *Unsecular Man: The Persistence of Religion*, New York: Delta 1972

Handbook of the Ulster Question, North Eastern Boundary Bureau 1923

Harbinson, J. F., *The Ulster Unionist Party*, Belfast: Blackstaff 1973

Harris, R., *Prejudice and Tolerance in Ulster*, Manchester University Press 1972

Hepburn, A. C., *The Conflict of Nationality in Modern Ireland*, London: Edward Arnold 1980

Hepburn, A. C., *Minorities in History*, London: Edward Arnold 1978

Herberg, W., *Protestant, Catholic, Jew*, New York: Anchor, 1960

Hickey, J., 'Religion and the Analysis of the Northern Ireland Conflict', *Social Studies*, vol. 6, no. 3, 1977

Hickey, J., 'Religion, Values and Everyday Life. A Case Study in Northern Ireland', *CISR*, vol. 16, Paris 1981

Hickey, J., *Urban Catholics*, London: Geoffrey Chapman 1967

Insight (*Sunday Times*), *Ulster*, London, André Deutsch 1972

Jackson, J. A., *The Irish in Britain*, London: Routledge and Kegan Paul 1963

Johnson, B., 'Sociological Theory and Religious Truth', *Sociological Analysis*, vol. 38, no. 4, 1977

Larkin, E., 'The Devotional Revolution in Ireland, 1850-1875', *American Historical Review*, lxxvii, 3 June 1972

Laslett, P., *The World We Have Lost*, London University Paperbacks 1965

Leyton, E., *The One Blood: Kinship and Class in an Irish Village*, Memorial University of Newfoundland 1975

Lijphart, A., 'The Northern Ireland Problem: Cases, Theories and Solutions', *British Journal of Political Science*, vol. 5, 1975, pp. 83-106

Luckmann, T., *The Invisible Religion*, New York: Macmillan 1967

Lyons, F. S. L., *Ireland since the Famine*, London: Fontana 1973

Lyons, F. S. L., *Culture and Anarchy in Ireland 1890-1939*, Oxford: Clarendon Press 1979

Maduro, O., 'New Marxist Approaches to the Relative Autonomy of Religion', *Sociological Analysis*, vol. 38, no. 4, 1977

Martin, D., *A General Theory of Secularization*, Oxford: Blackwell 1978

Martin, D., *A Sociology of English Religion*, London: Heinemann 1967

Mehl, R., *The Sociology of Protestantism*, London: SCM 1970

Miller, D. W., *Queen's Rebels*, Dublin: Gill and Macmillan 1978

Moody, T. W., *The Ulster Question, 1603-1973*, Cork: Mercier 1974

Newman Review, The, *Bibliography of Contemporary Writing on Northern Ireland*, Summer 1970

Northern Friends Peace Board, *Orange and Green*, NFPB 1969

O'Brien, C. C., *States of Ireland*, London: Hutchinson 1972

O'Farrell, P., *England and Ireland since 1800*, OUP 1975

O'Farrell, P., *Ireland's English Question*, New York: Schocken 1971

Parsons, T., *Action Theory and the Human Condition*, New York: Free Press 1978

Robertson, R., *The Sociological Interpretation of Religion*, Oxford: Blackwell 1970

Rose, R., *Governing without Consensus: An Irish Perspective*, London: Faber and Faber, 1971

Rose, R., *Northern Ireland: A Time of Choice*, London: Macmillan 1976

Rumpf. E. and A. C. Hepburn, *Nationalism and Socialism in Twentieth Century Ireland*, Liverpool University Press 1977

Russell, J., 'Northern Ireland: Socialization into Conflict', *Social Studies, Irish Journal of Sociology*, vol. 4, no. 2, 1975

Sectarianism — Roads to Reconciliation, Dublin: Three Candles Press 1974

Stewart, A. T. Q., *The Ulster Crisis*, London: Faber 1967

Stewart, A. T. Q., *The Narrow Ground*, London: Faber 1977

Suttles, J., *The Social Order of the Slum*, University of Chicago Press 1968

Target, G., *Unholy Smoke*, London: Hodder and Stoughton 1969

Tawney, R. H., *Religion and the Rise of Capitalism*, Harmondsworth, Mdx: Penguin 1948 edn.

Towler, R., *Homo Religiosus: Sociological Problems in the Study of Religion*, London: Constable 1974

Turner, J., 'Marx and Simmel Revisited; Re-assessing the Foundations of Conflict Theory', *Social Forces*, vol. 53, no. 4, 1975

Wach, J., *The Sociology of Religion*, University of Chicago Press 1944

Wallace, M., *Drums and Guns: Revolution in Ulster*, London: Geoffrey Chapman 1970

Weber, M., *The Protestant Ethic and the Spirit of Capitalism*, New York: Scribners 1958

Weber, M., 'The Social Psychology of the World Religions' in H. Gerth and C. W. Mills, *From Max Weber*, OUP 1968 edn.

Weber, M., *The Sociology of Religion*, London: Methuen 1965

Wells, R. A. and B. S. Mawhinney, *Conflict and Christianity in Northern Ireland*, Michigan: Erdmans 1975

Whyte, J. H., *Church and State in Modern Ireland*, Dublin: Gill and Macmillan 1971

Whyte, J. H., 'Interpretations of the Northern Ireland Problem: An Appraisal', *Economic and Social Review*, vol. ix, no. 4, July 1978

Wilson, B., *Contemporary Transformations of Religion*, Oxford: Clarendon Press 1979

Wilson, B., *Religion in Secular Society*, Harmondsworth, Mdx: Penguin 1966

Wright, F., 'Protestant Ideology and Politics in Ulster', *European Journal of Sociology*, vol. xiv, no. 2, 1973, pp. 213-80

Index

Acquaviva, S. S., 106, 107-8
Alliance Party, 103
Antrim, 13, 45
Apprentice Boys, 15, 25
Ardoyne, 15
Armagh, 13

Beckett, J. C., 18
Belfast, 13, 14, 15-20, 25, 98, 99, 100, 137
Belfast City Council, 19
Bew, P., *et al.*, 49, 52-3, 54
Blaxter, L., *et al.*, 4
Bogside, 25
Borhek, J. F. and R. F. Curtis, 59, 60
Boundary Commission, 11-12
British Army, 10, 25, 33
British 'imperialism', 36, 90, 125

Campaign for Social Justice, 23
Catholicism, Catholics *see under* Roman Catholicism
'Carson Trail', 46
Catholic Convention, 17
Cavan, 6
Centre for the Study of Conflict (New University of Ulster), 4
Church of Ireland, 13, 63, 68-70
Clann na hÉireann, 37
clergy *see* Protestantism and Roman Catholicism
Coleraine, 15, 45, 99
conflict: explanations of, 29ff., 79; interpretations, 56-60
Connaught, 5
Conservative Party, British, 10
Council of Ireland, 10-11
'cultural nationalism', 39-40

Darby, J., 4, 29

Democratic Unionist Party (DUP), 45
Derry: city, 14, 15, 100, 137, 138; county, 13
Dewer, Dr M. W., 77-8
direct rule, 26
Dissenting Protestants, 70
Donegal, 6
Down, County, 6, 13
Dublin government, 44
Dublin Summit, 45
Durkheim, E., 111

Education Act 1947, 22

Falls, the, Belfast, 15, 25
'false consciousness', 54, 55-6
Farrell, M., 49, 50-1, 54-5
Faulkner, B., 126
Fermanagh, 14
Free Presbyterians, 13, 74

Gaelic Athletic Association (GAA), 39-40
ghetto, Belfast Catholic, 16
Gladstone, W. E., 7
Government of Ireland Act (1920), 10
grace, interpretations of 69-70
Greeley, A. M., 106-7, 108

Harris, R., 4
H Block campaign, 36, 103
Haughey, C., 44
Hepburn, A. C., 19, 149
Home Rule, 6-8, 9
Hughes, B., 19
hunger strike, 36, 47
Hyde, D., 41

'individualisation', 94, 95-96
internment, 26

Irish culture, 39-43
Irish Free State, 11
Irish nationalism, 6, 11-13, 27
Irish Republican Army (IRA): 2, 22-3, 24, 124, 125; Official, 26; Provisional, 26, 44, 47, 51

James II, 15, 64, 138

'Labour aristocracy', 49-50
Larkin, E., 143
Leinster, 5
Lemass, S., 23
Leyton, E., 4
Liberal Party, British, 7-8
Lloyd George, D., 8
Londonderry, County, 13, *see also* Derry
Lyons, F. S. L., 39, 149

Marx, Karl, 48
Marxist interpretation, 27, 30, 48-56, 59, 89, 90, 109, 120
Mehl, R., 63, 150
Methodists, 13, 63
Miller, D., 123-4, 150
mixed marriages, 103, 138-9
'modernisation', 28, 93-4, 96-8, 102, 104-5, 126
Monaghan, County, 6
Moran, D. P., 41, 42
Munster, 5

National Assistance and Health Services Act (1948), 22
'Nationalist' interpretation, 31-3, 89, 90, 120
Northern Ireland Civil Rights Association (NICRA), 24-5
Northern Ireland Constitution Act (1972), 26
Northern Ireland Labour Party (NILP), 1, 50

O'Connell, Daniel, 19
O'Farrell, P., 71-3, 150
O'Neill, Terence, Prime Minister Northern Ireland, 23, 25, 72, 124
Orange Order, 50, 63, 64-6, 67, 77-8, 101
Orange Standard, 87-8

Paisley, Rev. Ian, 13, 24, 45-6, 64, 67, 68, 73, 74-5, 78, 124, 126
Parsons, T., 70
Party Emblems Act 1860, 20
Party Processions Act 1850, 20
People's Democracy, 25
'politico-cultural explanation', 27, 30
population, 13, 30, 99
Portstewart, 99
Portrush, 99
Presbyterians, 13, 63, 77
priesthood, 69
Protestant culture, 43, 67
Protestant Telegraph, 67, 73, 74, 87
Protestantism: clergy, 63-4, 70, 76, 85-6; diversity of, 63, 75-6, 79; future of in Northern Ireland, 70, 85; future of in Republic of Ireland, 71, 73, 77, 85, 88; political differences with Roman Catholicism, 64, 70, 71, 72-4, 75-6, 79, 80; survival of, 72-4, 85-7; other references, 63-4, 82

race relations model, 29-30
religion: decline of, 59, 106-114; future of, 106-114; link with other institutions, 59, 62, 63, 64, 66, 71; link with politics, 65-6, 67, 71; political significance of, 58-9, 64, 71; treatment of, 60-3; *see also* Protestantism and Roman Catholicism
Republican Clubs, 36
Republican interpretation, 33-8, 89, 90, 120
Republican News, 36
riots and rioting, 20, 21, 25
Robinson, P., 45
Roman Catholicism: clergy, 69, 76, 77, 84, 86; in Northern Ireland, 69; political differences with Northern Ireland Protestantism, 70-6, 80; in Republic of Ireland, 84-7
Rose, R., 4
Royal Ulster Constabulary, 21, 47

Sands, B., 48
sectarian violence, 3, 14, 20, 21-2, 26, 118-19
secularisation, 94-5
Shankill, 25

Sinn Féin, Official, 37; Provisional, 36, 37; other references, 8, 26
Smyth, Rev. M., 69, 75-7, 87
Social Democratic and Labour Party (SDLP), 34-5
'Solemn League and Covenant', 9
'State' of Northern Ireland, 21
Stormont, 10, 14
Sunday Times, 46
survey methodology, 4, 127

Thatcher, M., 44, 46
'two cultures' interpretation, 38-43, 91-2, 120
Tyrone, County, 13

Ulster, 5-6
Ulster Defence Association (UDA), 51
Ulster Volunteer Force (UVF): in 1912, 10; present-day, 23-4, 26, 51
Ulster Workers' Council, 74, 126
Unionism, 27, 101
Unionists, 8-13, 64-6, 101, 121

Weber, M., 62-3, 82, 150, 151
Westminster, 7, 8, 9, 11, 22, 26, 35, 38, 44, 45, 123
Whyte, J., 29, 48-9, 151
William of Orange, 64
Wilson, B., 107, 108-9, 151